You're Not a Burden

How I Came to Realize There Are No Limits to
How Much Love a Heart Can Hold

Kathleen A. Nawojczyk

ISBN 978-1-0980-9021-0 (paperback)
ISBN 978-1-0980-9023-4 (hardcover)
ISBN 978-1-0980-9022-7 (digital)

Christian Faith Publishing, Inc.
832 Park Avenue
Meadville, PA 16335
www.christianfaithpublishing.com

Printed in the United States of America

I dedicate this book to my Danny.

I will always remember your embraces, as having your strong arms wrapped around me provided the feeling of contentment and safety. I would often tell you that being snuggled in your arms made me feel as though the world around us could fall apart; but as long as your arms were around me, no harm would come to us.

Thank you for many years of laughter, as you were the funniest and wittiest man I've ever known.

Thank you for bringing out the little girl in me often enough that I never forgot her and for sharing with me the little boy in you.

You enriched my life immeasurably and I thank God for loaning you to me.

Through the process of writing this book, I have been emotionally emptied and I have been emotionally filled, both adding much to these writings and both necessary for this story to be truly felt.

Acknowledgments

To my Lord and Savior, Jesus Christ, who guides me daily and heals the brokenhearted.

To my mother-in-law, Irene Nawojczyk, who embraces life and all it has to offer and for your delightful, sprightly sense of humor.

To my sisters, Marylou Candiloro and Judy Valvano, my niece, Marissa Quay and my brother-in-law and sister-in-law, Ron and Monica Nawojczyk, for your raw and honest critique, which heartened me.

To my brother-in-law, Raymond Candiloro, for your gallant care, for being there for me in so many ways (knee surgery, among other appointments), and for being the best Uber Eats deliverer ever.

To Pastor Lloyd and Karen Pulley...there are no words to adequately express my gratitude. And Lloyd, the message you delivered at Danny's service was powerful and timely.

To all who prayed and gave selflessly in so many ways: my family, friends, church family, my work family, and the ladies in my Bible study, I truly wish I could name you all, but I fear leaving even one person out...you all know who you are and may God bless you all tenfold.

To Tom Hall, having a boss so incredibly compassionate and supportive was more than I could have ever hoped for. I had no work stress because you understood all too well what we were facing.

To my niece, Veronica Upchurch, for coming up with the title of this book in under ten seconds...your insight is extraordinary!

To Jon Flanagan, the great care you took with my Danny will always be remembered. Even when it came to separating his ashes, you were so thoughtful, so caring. You are in the job you were meant for.

❖ "You've written a heartfelt memoir of honest raw emotion, with a focus on the value of faith, friendship, family, gratitude, humor and hope."

—Marylou Candiloro

❖ "It sucked me right in. Really well written (so relatable)... I truly look forward to the finished product. It will be an amazing work of love."

—Roberto (Bert) Herrera

❖ "Your story is so beautifully honest, heartfelt, and compelling. I really enjoyed reading it... I could hear your voice so distinctly as I read."

—Monica Nawojczyk

When things go sideways in life or we receive bad news, my motto has been, "It could be worse, at least it's not a cancer diagnosis." But what happens when it is a cancer diagnosis?

Thank you for joining me, as I share our journey through life while my husband battled cancer. This is not from the viewpoint of a caregiver, but from a wife who loved her husband and needed him to know that he was not alone in this fight and *that he was not a burden.* When I began writing, it was envisioned to be a story of inspiration and triumph over cancer. I was so sure he was going to beat it; I never foresaw any other scenario. In light of that, I believe it will still speak to all who read it, no matter your perspective.

To those of you who have a loved one fighting a mighty disease or a terminal illness, I implore you to not let them see the pain you're feeling because of the pain they are suffering. It is so difficult to watch; it's cruel really. This commission is not for the faint of heart, as you must persevere. I loved my husband with more love than I imagined my heart held, and I take great solace, as I saw the gratitude in his beautiful warm brown eyes every day. You will never regret showering them with all the love and compassion you have. Try to never let them see your heartache, as it hurts them more than you know.

November 2017: 353 East 68th Street, New York City

As I stand looking out the examination room window to the playground below on this chilly November morning, I feel like I'm in the opening scene of a major motion picture. New York City playgrounds are different from suburban playgrounds. They're surrounded by high-rise apartments, brownstones, businesses, and hospitals. I see a dad and his little boy running around, seemingly not a care in the world; and on the opposite end of the playground are a couple of nannies with their charges, who they half watch while they text. I turn back to see my husband sitting on the chair against the wall, puffing on his e-cigarette. I shake my head and do the eye roll and can't help but smile because he is who he is, and I love him to pieces. I sit down next to him and put my hand on his hand.

The nurse comes in to go over everything with us…Sally. I like her, she's kind, but straightforward. She sits across the room from us at her computer. She has a lot of questions for Danny that we will come to find out she will ask him at every visit going forward. Then she comes over and sits down in front of us and begins going over what Danny *will* experience and what he *might* experience with the chemo treatments. The list seems infinite, and my stomach is starting to hurt. And I turn my head slightly to capture a look in his eyes that seems to be wondering, as am I, when is it going to end? His soulful, soft brown eyes tell so much; they always have. The tears silently spill from my eyes and Sally gets up to get me tissues. He looks over at me surprised to see me crying. I looked up at him and said, "I'm sorry. It's just so much." Sally agrees it's a lot to take in. That's putting it mildly. It's not the perpetual list as much as what my husband may or may not go through when he's already gone through so much.

It All Began One Day in September

The path that brought us to this point had all the elements of an amusement park ride with one exception; there is nothing amusing about it. It was early *September 2017* when Danny mentioned he felt his kidney stones were back. I suggested he see the urologist right away before the pain gets too intense. The urologist confirmed he did have kidney stones; however, they weren't in an area of the kidney that they should be causing him pain, which left us to wonder, is that good or bad? Three guesses. Exploratory surgery was scheduled; and while unable to confirm until the biopsy results came back, the doctor was pretty sure it was cancer, although he couldn't say just yet.

The day after that exploratory surgery, Danny called me at work to tell me he was in a lot of pain. I was certain it was gas from the anesthesia and his doctor confirmed that. The following day he was still in a lot of pain. I still felt it was trapped gas; however, I'm a big proponent of everyone knowing their own bodies so I felt if he thought we should go to the hospital, then we should go, which is what we did. Thankfully we were taken in from the waiting room quickly and then waited in the hallway as opposed to sitting in the waiting room for hours, then being taken into the hallway and waiting again (I see this as a positive, more visibility).

After an hour or so, they were ready to do a CAT Scan that would take about two hours, so I thought I'd walk to the ShopRite because there were things Danny needed and it was just down the road, about a mile or so. I had flat shoes on so no problem. I hadn't considered the tricky course, as I had to take Broad Street in Summit down to Morris Avenue in Springfield. Who knew there were no sidewalks in some areas. Oh well, I already committed to the walk, so I asked myself, "What's the worst-case scenario?" It wasn't pretty, but I'd be careful and so I carried on. I made it there and back just in time to find them wheeling him back from the CAT scan. Shortly thereafter we're told he has perforated diverticulitis. Are you kidding us!?! To say we were blindsided would be an understatement; and unfortunately, this was just the beginning of the blindsides. The cause was unrelated to the exploratory surgery he had just two days earlier, and emergency surgery had to be scheduled that night. They finally had a room ready for him and we waited. A resident doctor came in and was going over everything to do with the surgery. As I'm listening, I'm observing Danny, and I'm thinking, "Will he need to have an ostomy?"

When I asked the resident, he said there was a 60 percent chance he wouldn't, but Danny was thinking, "There's a 40 percent chance I will." And I could see the terror in his eyes. He became very anxious as did I, but I wouldn't show it. We asked the resident to give us a few minutes. When he left the room, Danny looked at me with this horrified look on his face and told me he can't do this. Suddenly, I was so angry that this resident just delivered this troubling news with little more than a shrug of his shoulders and basically told us we had no choice. I looked at Danny and told him we must trust God. There's no time for a second opinion. As it turned out, the surgeon told us that yes, he would need to have an ostomy, but that it would be temporary and they would reverse it in a few months. Now my only thought is to hunt down that resident and smack him right upside his head…insensitive dolt!

Thankfully, my sister-in-law stayed with me the entire time. We were there past midnight, both of us cold and tired, and our contacts were starting to fog up. I remember telling her how I realized I'm one of those people who sweat the small stuff. Like when my husband gets a speeding ticket, I lose it, because now our insurance will go up, or the dishwasher breaks down, and we didn't opt to get the extra insurance. However, when it comes to the big stuff, I'm all in and will do whatever is needed of me and then some.

The surgery was a success and I was so eager to tell him. So when he woke up and I told him all was well, he just stared at me. I thought to myself, he thinks he's dreaming; and sure enough, that's what he told me the next day. He remembered me telling him, but he thought he was dreaming. That's okay, so I drove home with foggy contacts. I'd do it all over again just to deliver good news, whether he comprehended it or not.

As if he needed another challenge, he contracted *C. difficile*… this poor man. They had to clear the floor due to the high contamination risk to other patients, and Danny saw this as a positive. He said, "Now I can get a nurse anytime, without having to wait." Oh, how I love my "glass-half-full husband!"

A few days later I went to my second cousin's, Leanne's, wedding…with Danny's blessing (he loves Leanne and so wished he could have gone). I had been looking forward to this wedding, but I didn't think I'd be going without Danny. Leanne did the sweetest thing. Knowing he couldn't be there, to lighten things up for me, she had our seating card changed from "Mr. & Mrs. Daniel Nawojczyk" to "Cool Aunt Kathy" (which is how she often referred to me), and it certainly lifted my spirits. I managed to enjoy myself, but it saddened me when the slow songs played. I would have loved to have danced with my man.

Which brought to mind the time we danced to the song "Crazy," by Patsy Cline in our living room while watching *Doc Hollywood*, because that song played in a scene in that movie. I just had to dance with him. He reluctantly agreed, since it meant he'd have to get up from his big, comfy chair, but after a minute he was into it.

The very first song we ever danced to was "Unchained Melody." We were at the first wedding we'd ever been to together; and that was the first slow song they played...a timeless, beautiful song. I just thought I'd share that.

Dealing with Cancer

The results of the biopsy came back; my Danny has cancer.

It suddenly hits me; God has entrusted him in my care. Me! This is no small thing. I looked at it this way: I get to take care of him, to encourage him, and to be his biggest cheerleader (without being obnoxious). These days a cancer diagnosis is not a death sentence and I couldn't emphasize that enough. I also told him two things that I would remind him of throughout this ride. I told him to *always* remember, "You're not alone, and *you're not a burden*!" There has not been a challenge in our lives that we haven't risen together to face. This one will be no different.

To See the Dichotomy

Early in our marriage, I found out Danny was addicted to cocaine. We didn't live together before we got married, so he was able to easily keep me in the dark. After going to secular rehabs, we were told about a Christian rehab in South Jersey, America's Keswick, and there he went...twice.

The second time when he relapsed in his addiction, my friend Dee-Dee was battling inflammatory breast cancer. Her husband was at America's Keswick the same time as Danny, the first time, so she knew what living with an addicted husband was like. I will never forget what she said to me when she found out he relapsed. She said, "Kath, I feel for you that you have to go through this again. I'd rather have cancer." And she meant it. I remembered I gasped, as I was taken back by what she said, but then understood.

When someone you love makes bad, life-altering choices that could ruin their lives or, worse, kill them, it's devastating; and those bad choices also bring you down, down to a low you never thought you could be brought down to. You resent them and you almost hate them. My love for my husband outweighed my hate for his bad choices so I stood by him and prayed desperately for him. My love for Jesus and thinking about what He did for me on the cross helped significantly.

When your husband is dealing with a disease, like cancer, you will do anything to show him he is not alone and you will fight alongside him with every fiber of your being, and more love and compassion that you didn't even know you had emerges from you. When watching him in pain and seeing the sadness in his eyes, I would fall to my knees and beg God to take his pain away because it's so incredibly agonizing to watch. Then I reflect on the fact that God watched his only son die the most horrific death, for the entire human race... and I get a slight glimpse of what he experienced, and I am humbled.

Interjected Thought #1: The Dichotomy Revealed

I believe people can be predisposed to succumbing to drug addiction, alcoholism, etc. I don't believe addiction is a disease (and no, I don't care what the world thinks). I've lived with both. And one is clearly a disease and the other is clearly a bad choice. Folks don't choose to get cancer, so it's distressing when they choose that which can destroy them. The good news is there is no stigma attached to bad choices, which helps the addict feel less shame and less defeated, which, in turn, will help them face their addiction with a more hopeful mindset.

Upsides and Downsides

There have been upsides along the way, one being I can still drive in the city as good as I used to. In my twenties I drove fearlessly in the city; but it's been awhile, so I was a bit intimidated. Not having an option, I had to suck it up and drive in until they were able to schedule him in the MSK Basking Ridge, New Jersey, facility. Driving home one night, the GPS directed us through Times Square; this was during the height of the Christmas season. Imagine the stimulation to our senses, the neon lights, the flashing billboards, and the tourists coming at us from all sides, surrounding my silver Mini Cooper. I told Danny I felt as though we were driving around on a pinball machine! It was exhilarating. He agreed. We were thoroughly enjoying this, forgetting for just a few minutes why we were even there. And by the way, Danny was very impressed at my NYC driving skills. I was a maniac at times; I had to be because when driving in the city it's eat or be eaten!

The Toll It Takes

At times I didn't realize the toll this was taking on us. I'm going along one day at a time, doing what needs to be done, being there for Danny, and going to work. I also have a part-time job teaching spin and weight/cardio classes at the YMCA. Then when one small, insignificant thing is said, and my brain explodes, and I said things I didn't mean. I then look to God and plead with him to help me fix this. This just happened and I said things that didn't even make sense because I was so tired (not that that's an excuse, although it sort of is). And my words hurt him and I apologized, crying uncontrollably.

Then he was crying; and we told each other how sorry we were, letting each other know how much we love each other, him telling me how he feels bad I have so much to do and me telling him I don't care about me. I needed him to know I love him and reminded him he is not alone and *he is not a burden*. Then he reached out and hugged me and that was so healing. And I cherish the feeling of those still strong, loving arms around me. I told him how I think about him the minute I leave the house and throughout the day and how I could kick myself when the other day I looked at him and told him to "have a good day." Ugh, I sat in my car and admonished myself, what an idiot I was for telling him to have a good day. I'm starting to rethink using this phrase, because today it feels hollow to me.

The ups and downs of this disease are bringing us closer together (I didn't think we could get any closer). Also, I have cried more in the last few months than I have in the last few years, no exaggeration. You find yourself going through the motions, doing what you need to do, and sometimes you almost forget to breath. You wake up every morning, for the first couple of months forgetting for just a few seconds what's going on; and then you exhale, as you remember.

A New Day

Today he started the first chemo treatment of the third cycle; and when I called him to see how he was feeling, it was music to my ears. He sounded wonderful and my heart leaped with joy. These are the days I cherish, and I thank my loving God for them. We had a nice evening; we laughed and hugged. I loved today.

The entire week turned out to be a good one for Danny, and I am grateful beyond measure. He went fishing yesterday, as we had a break from the cold. And it was a beautiful Saturday in January. Today is Sunday, January 21; and as I was leaving for church this morning, he was just waking up.

I Digress for a Good Reason

I love being a greeter at church. My friend, Linda, walks in with pure honey from her farm (she knows I've been making tea with honey, fresh ginger, and lemon for Danny). She is such a blessing to me; and I know she and her husband, Wayne, are one of the many people praying for us. We had a guest speaker, Pastor Wes Bentley, from *Far Reaching Ministries*. Wow, this sermon was so unexpected. He spoke about the persecution of Christians in South Sudan. To hear what he had to say was gut-wrenching. I, and mostly everyone, was in tears as we listened intently to what these persecutors do to infants, children, and Christians of all ages. It is unspeakable, unfathomable, and unconscionable. How humans can be so inhumane is incomprehensible. Their hatred for Christians is merciless. What this man has seen you cannot conceive of. I texted Danny after the service and asked him if he saw it. He watched via livestream…he cried too.

I mention this because while on this journey, I believe God wants me to be mindful that there are so many people going through so much, clearly some much worse and others not as bad, but they all need prayer.

And We're Back

This Tuesday Danny was supposed to get his second treatment in the third cycle, but his white cell count was too low, so they were unable to administer it. They gave him a white blood cell stimulate to boost his count, but the side effects were terribly unsettling. He thought he was having a heart attack and it was causing back spasms. The next few days were extremely unpleasant for him. His brother Jimmy came over to help repair a couple of things, and they ended up hanging out and having a nice time together which boosted his spirits.

SBS: 2018

This coming weekend is Super Bowl Sunday. We have a small gathering, his mom, his sister, and anyone else who wants to join. Danny is thrilled that his nieces, Candace and Casey, want to come over. I was going to mention it to them when they came to visit a few weeks back, but I didn't want them to feel obligated. So, you can imagine how happy we were that they wanted to spend it with us. We love that they enjoy being at our home. Danny made New York

Strip Steaks and twice-baked potatoes for everyone, yum. He outdid himself once again for SBS and a good time was had by all.

Persevering Through More Challenges

This week he got through his treatment and I noticed he wasn't as wiped out as usual. He also got the flu shot and the pneumococcal phenomena shot, which were crucial since his immune system is compromised. It's been another good week. Praise God. He's making pizza tonight; I'm so happy. I love his pizza; it's the best.

Fast forward from January to May. Yes, I've been MIA for a couple of months. There have been so many issues in between...far too many to list. May 14, 2018, he had his kidney removed and the ostomy closed. The eight-hour surgery went well in both areas, but the pathology report would tell a more accurate story.

Often there are kind folks who bring their dogs as a comfort to those at MSK. This Cavalier King Charles Spaniel was a cutie and a nice surprise for Danny. How cute are they?

During this week while he was in the hospital, I stayed overnight the first night then traveled in daily, by bus, with my friend, Estrella, who works in the city. What a blessing. One of the evenings when she was done with work, we grabbed a bite to eat and then had gelato. It was a much-needed respite.

The report came back showing the two lymph nodes that were removed along with the left kidney which showed live cancer cells, which means there's a 90 percent chance the cancer would return. But, there's a 10 percent chance it won't (ever the optimist). Six weeks later we received the devastating news that the cancer had returned. After getting through the surgery and the intense pain of the incision, he was good for a few weeks. Good enough to play golf…I was so happy for him. However, the freedom from pain was not to last. In addition to the news that the cancer returned, he was experiencing the same pain in the same place where the kidney was. The pain seemed worse after his golf game and it's not getting better. He made an appointment to see the surgical oncologist.

Back to New York City, the morning of *July 24, 2018*. I dropped him off at the hospital, parked the car, and stopped by my favorite café. Yes, I now have a favorite New York City café. They make their own bagels, and Danny loves bagels. Meeting went well, as they determined the pain is due to musculoskeletal issues. The muscles that surrounded the eradicated kidney were prodded, causing trauma to the area. The golf game didn't help.

We have been blessed by the prayers of many, some who we will never meet. I always ask God to bless all who are praying for us in the ways they need it most, and I have no doubt he has or he will. In addition to prayers, family and friends have provided for us in countless ways, which helps make life less stressful. Words cannot adequately express our gratitude for all that has been done for us.

Someone recently sent me a message that said, "Maybe you've been assigned this mountain to show others it can be moved." I suspect God's unrevealed plan is in motion.

God continues to carry me and strengthen me, and he pours his gift of peace in me daily. The song "Good Good Father" by Chris Tomlin says it all.

Wednesday, October 17, 2018: Again, it's been a few months since I've added to our story. We continue to ride this roller coaster together. I had a tough time sitting down and inviting you to continue with me. I just didn't feel like writing. The thought of it was daunting. I think because I'm feeling alone today. But as I was watching the news this morning, Ainsley Earhardt was interviewing Pastor Andrew Brunson who was just released from a prison in Turkey after two years. His wife spoke at our church some time ago and I was in awe of her faith, strength, and courage. Their faith touched my heart and reminded me that no matter what is happening in our lives, God is with us, even if we don't feel like he is. I need to remember this because another blindside is coming.

Before I get to that, I would like you to become a bit more acquainted with Danny, as there are many unique qualities that make up the character of this man of mine.

- ❖ In a book that was given to his mom, by his sister, Diana, entitled *Grandma's Daily Book of Memories*, one of the things she wrote when asked how she approached the subject of "the birds and the bees" with her children was this story about Danny: "One day I said to Danny I want to talk to you about the birds and bees. And he said, 'what do you want to know?'"
- ❖ When he was being reprimanded by his kindergarten teacher, he interrupted her to tell her how pretty she looked in the dress she was wearing…he was five years old!
- ❖ One Saturday I went to a convention with the ladies in my Bible study. That same day, Danny attended the men's breakfast (this was at our former church). I left my car at the church and drove to the convention with a couple of the other ladies. When I returned I found this note on my windshield:

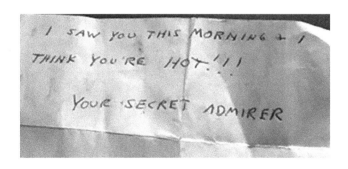

Oh how it made me laugh. I love unexpected surprises like this, more than flowers. When I got home I told him I got his note. He pretended not to know what I was talking about. Besides knowing his printing, I asked him if he really wanted me to think some guy from our church, of all places, who knows we're married, put this note on my car. He laughed and said, "Huh, I didn't think that through." That was easily sixteen years ago, if not more. I still have the note and it still makes me laugh.

❖ We often communicated using Bitmojis. I have an album on my iPhone full of Bitmojis he sent me.

One day he asked me why I saved them, and I told him because they make me laugh. He asked to see the album and he was in tears, laughing (he had the best laugh). Once he composed himself, he said, "I'm pretty funny!"

When I hadn't received one in a long time, I told him I missed his Bitmojis, so he sent me this...

❖ You didn't have to know Danny to love him. There are people in my life who loved him without ever having met him, because of the many "Danny" stories I would tell. There was even a Team Danny where I work, which was started by my friends and coworkers, Sherrell and Yvette. Whenever he would call to tell me he needed money, they would hear me on the phone asking him why he needs more money; and they would chant, "Team Danny, Team Danny." He loved that. While Sherrell and her husband, Reggie, did know him, as we got together with them for dinners and barbeques, my friend, Yvette, never got to meet him. He so wanted to meet her and, in his words, give her a big hug. You see, it was Yvette and Sherrell who were responsible for taking up the collections for us at work. It was so amazing, and I will always be humbled by this expression of friendship and love.

❖ He had friends that he hadn't been in touch with for a few decades. Not even via social media. When a couple of them heard he was sick, they traveled up from Florida to visit him in the hospital. He was most humbled; and he said to me, "I feel really loved." I told him I didn't know anyone who is more loved than him. It's true. He had good friends, because he was a genuine and good friend.

❖ Every now and then, he would still surprise me. While in the hospital, I asked him, as I usually did, if there was anything he wanted me to bring when I returned the next day. Among the items he listed, he asked me to bring his prayer list. I looked at him and said, "Your prayer list?"

He said, "You're not the only one who has a prayer list, you know."

To which I replied, "I know. I just thought I was the only one in our house that had a prayer list." He did the eyebrow raise as if to say, very funny.

Oh, the Games People Play

Throughout our marriage we often played games with each other. The one that stands out the most was the game phase of seeing who could scare the other the best. This went on for several years. The two most popular hiding places were the stairs going up to the second floor and the other was behind the front door. That was the best because there are no sidelights or windows in the door.

So one day I parked my car and headed up the walkway. Across the street, Isabella, who was only about six years old at the time, kept popping up in her window and saying, "boo," then ducking below the window. So I kept saying, "I see you." This went on between her and I about five times. And when I finally reached the front door, it flew open; and Danny looked at me, incredulously, and said, "How were you able to see me?" I had to stop and think for a second, not realizing what he was talking about; and then I just started laughing, barely able to explain. Then he started laughing, I think he was relieved that I couldn't see through doors! In hindsight, I really should have played that up.

We also played games while driving, like guessing who the band/singer was playing on the radio. If either of us had a brain freeze, we would give each other clues, which was the best part. For instance, one time his clue (during a time that he was out of work and money was tight) was, "What we're going through right now."

And I immediately said, "Oh, Dire Straits!" We laughed so hard. His clues were the best.

Tell Us How You Really Feel

One of the things I marveled at was how he could tell it like it is, without hurting your feelings. Because if you knew him, you knew he wasn't saying whatever it was with any malice. One example was when his brother, Jimmy, and his wife, Susan, bought a new house and we went to visit. We walked into the foyer, which was relatively big; and Jim said, "So this is the foyer, and over there is the living room." The living room was a tiny slice of a room; and when Danny turned to look at it, he simply said, "Well there's a waste of space."

I thought to myself, "Wow, really Dan."

But his brother just shrugged and said, "I know, right?" If I had said that it would have come out so wrong. But Jimmy understood this and thought nothing of it. It's a gift few possess.

What stands out the most for me is that Danny was a kid magnet. He genuinely loved being around kids and they knew it. Kids are so in tune to who is genuine and who isn't, and I couldn't name a single child who wasn't drawn to my husband. It's too bad we weren't able to have children, because he would have been the best dad. He was so loved by all his nieces and nephews as well as by the kids in our neighborhood. Of all the kiddos in the neighborhood, he was especially close with Amelia. She would come over while I'd be gardening and ask where Dan was and proceed to walk into the house and hang out with him. When he became ill, whenever I saw her, she would always ask, "How's Dan?" It warmed my heart and broke my heart all at the same time.

With our niece, Veronica

Nieces and nephews: Cole, Mark, Casey, Candace, Dani Jo, and Connor

With Amelia

With our niece, Marissa

It is my hope that you have a better appreciation of what this unique husband of mine was like.

I suppose it's time now that I shared.

The Worst Blindside of All: October 2018

A month or so ago, we decided to try immunotherapy, which I had high hopes for. When we met with the oncologist to see how Danny was doing on it, I could not have been more unprepared. As she was talking, I found myself asking myself, "What is she saying?" It was as if I was listening to Charlie Brown's teacher. I told her I didn't understand why she was saying we should stop the immunotherapy. That's when Danny said, "She's telling us I'm dying."

I looked back at her about to say, "Tell him he's not dying." But before I could get a word out, she put her head down and simply said, "I'm so sorry." What? Why is she saying she's sorry? Just then I felt my world go black.

If he did nothing, he had four to six months. If he chose a new chemo, she couldn't tell us how much time that would buy. Danny made the decision to continue with a new chemotherapy. I always told him I would stand by whatever he chose. This is a decision only he could make. He never asked me my opinion. He didn't want to burden me with being a part of a decision that might come back to haunt me. I know I would have felt the same way. We had come so far; he had gone through so much, only to be told there are no more options…no more options…a phrase that I've heard one too many times. I try to sort this out; I try to get a grip. But there's nothing to hold onto except the still strong hands of this man I love so desperately.

We cried uncontrollably the whole way home. When we walked in the door, feeling pretty spent, he sat in his favorite oversized chair and just looked at me with his beautiful, expression-filled eyes. I asked him if he wanted to pretend things were normal and suggested we catch up on our shows. *NCIS: Los Angeles, Hawaii Five-O,* or *Bull*—these are our favorite shows to watch together. He simply said, "Okay." I love how we "get" each other. We embraced as we watched our shows, which was calming.

Suddenly, we were getting texts from our friends in the neighborhood. We have the most wonderful friends. It was us and four other couples: George and Estrella, Kalman and Gabbie, Jon and

Fran, and Ileana and Joe. We consider them nothing less than family. Apparently, the lottery, which we don't normally play, was unusually big so they were asking if everyone wanted to go in on it. I ignored the texts, and out of nowhere Danny said we should play. I looked at him inquisitively. He said, "Well I won't be around to enjoy it if we win. But hey, you will." I shook my head, and he shrugged his shoulders and gave a little laugh. Nobody needs to ever wonder why I love this man so much. Even with just having been given a terminal diagnosis, his sense of humor has not waned. Dear God, I do love him so.

Telling everyone this latest diagnosis was arduous, at best. They had no words, but no words were expected. I almost felt bad having to deliver such devastating news…almost. I'm still trying to process this myself.

Everyone was all in with us. I could not list all the things that were done for us, as there are just too many to count. We are supported by the most generous, the most selfless people. *You all know who you are.*

One Love

One of the most wonderful gifts given to us was from Danny's older brother, Ron, and his wife, Monica. They treated us to a week in Jamaica in January 2019. We have always enjoyed our times with them, and this was no different. The trip was scheduled around

Danny's chemo treatments, so we left on January 5. We had the most amazing time and it's all he talked about for weeks. It wasn't the extravagance of the gift as much as the time spent together with Ron and Monica that made it so incredibly special.

A Happy Day on the Links

Upon our return from Jamaica, he was doing well. I could see the chemo was taking its toll, but he persevered. He was able to enjoy Super Bowl Sunday and he did well through Easter, April 21, 2019. However, midway through Easter dinner, he had become very tired.

There were good days and not-so-good days, but the first Saturday in June he was up for playing golf with his good friend, Steve. Afterward, he called to tell me he played the best golf game! The excitement in his voice filled me with joy. I wondered for a moment if he could be cancer-free; he sounded that good. Even Steve called me to tell me how good he did. To add to my joy, he even rode his bike the next day. That was a wonderful two days.

Shortly thereafter, he became severely dehydrated, so we rushed to Atlantic Health Urgent Care only minutes from our home. He was delirious, and I was scared and crying. They took great care of him, but he needed to be hospitalized. At one point a kind, gentle nurse pulled me aside and asked if he had a living will. I stared at her for a few seconds before saying yes. I felt like I was going to fall apart. Once they had an ambulance ready to take him, I left to go put some things together that he would be needing. The minute I exited the building, I broke down. The only person I thought to call was my friend, Kim, who lives in California. She answered on the first ring and was able to calm me down. Then in true Kim fashion, she actually had me laughing. Kim has a way of providing comic relief when you least expect it, but when you most need it. It's one of the many things I love her about her.

Leave the Gun, Take the Cannoli

I had never seen *The Godfather*; and this baffled Danny, as he could not believe this mortifying fact: his wife had never seen *The Godfather*. I'm not a mob movie person; what can I say. So, one dreary, rainy Saturday while he was in the hospital, I was straightening up his room; and as he was scrolling through the program guide on the TV, he saw that *The Godfather* was on and, get this, commercial-free! Well, he could not contain his excitement. It was quite adorable. He asked, "You wanna watch it don't you?" There was no way I would have said no. So, we snuggled in his hospital bed, as we often did and watched the movie.

I had to admit I enjoyed it. At one point, with our arms wrapped around each other, he kissed the top of my head, and I never want to forget what that felt like. There's something so special about being kissed on top of your head or forehead. It was as if he was telling me he was so happy to be sharing this day and this time together with just the two of us. At one point, a nurse came in to do something when out came the famous line in the movie, "Leave the gun, take the cannoli." She looked at the TV than at us and said, "Those Italians sure do have their priorities in order." We laughed. Being Italian myself, I couldn't agree more. Though I had managed to avoid seeing this movie for decades, there could not have been a better time to watch it together. I was happy that I did.

The Donning of the Wedding Dress

Every year on our anniversary, May 21, I put on my wedding dress. The idea to do this struck me when, after our wedding day, I was too cheap to have it preserved; besides, I didn't see the point. I didn't want to wear anyone's dress so, I thought, why would anyone want to wear mine?

Donning the dress every year gives me such joy because Danny always gets a kick out of it; and what's more, he forgets that I do this... *every year*! He remembers our anniversary, but not the dress (weird, I know). Over the years I have served him his morning coffee wearing it, I prepared dinner wearing it, and popped up out of nowhere while he was watching TV wearing it, on and on. One year I knew he would be home before me, so I brought the dress over to Kalman and Gabbie's the day before (Isabella and Amelia got such a kick out of that), and Gabbie called him to come over under some pretense. I don't recall what it was. But there I was, wearing my wedding gown!

However, this May 21, 2019, our twenty-fifth wedding anniversary, he was in the hospital (extremely low blood pressure and they were also working on getting his meds under control). Would I wear the dress to the hospital? No, I'm fun, not crazy. But I did bring it to the hospital in the big black trash bag that I kept it in (it stayed surprisingly white throughout the years); and, at the suggestion of my friend, Laura, I also brought two champagne glasses and Izze drinks, which he enjoys. Plan in motion.

He called me that morning and said, "If I'm not mistaken, honey. Isn't this our twenty-fifth anniversary?" I said, yes and told him I couldn't wait to see him, hoping not to reveal I was up to something and I remember thinking, "Of all the years to remember that I put on the dress, he'll remember this year." But he didn't...

On my way to the hospital, I ask God to please let this go smoothly. God one-upped me. When I arrived at the hospital and explained to the nurses what I wanted to do, they were all in. This was the oncology floor; not much in the way of fun happens there. They helped me with the dress; and one of the sweet nurses took the champagne glasses and my phone, which had our wedding song cued up, "Everything I do, I Do It for You," and proceeded to walk to his room. When she opened the door, he couldn't see me because the bed curtain was drawn; but in my line of sight, much to my surprise, was his brother, Ron. The look on his face when he saw me standing there in my wedding gown was priceless. He had no idea we do this every year, but thankfully he had the presence of mind to start video-taping. For this I will always be grateful.

When the nurse told Danny he had a visitor, I could hear the confusion in his voice, not knowing what to make of the champagne glasses and our song playing. When I stepped in so he could see me, well, my heart swelled with delight. He was so happy and so astonished! If you listen closely to the video, he laughingly asked, "What is wrong with you?" To which I replied, "Many things." You see, throughout our marriage, whenever he did something questionable/dumb, I would ask, "What is wrong with you?" And his reply was almost always, "Many things."

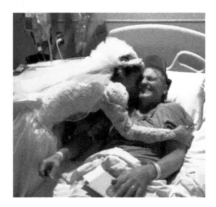

He was so happy. He told me he could not believe I had gone through so much trouble. I told him it was no trouble at all. There was never a thought that I wouldn't do this just because he was in the hospital. And now I have his joy-filled laugh captured on video forever, and that is a priceless gift. Yes, God certainly one-upped me.

The video can be viewed on the attached link, or you can type in "Wife Wears Wedding Dress To Surprise Husband In Hospital & Keep Up 25 Year Tradition."

https://www.youtube.com/watch?v=Sim8gMwKib8&t=9s

Our trip to Jamaica and the donning of the wedding dress were the two things that happened in 2019 that he spoke of most often. And when he did, a sweet smile appeared in his smiling eyes that warmed my heart.

The Worst Hostess/The Best Caretaker

Have you ever been at a house party where the hostess was stressed out, trying to make sure everyone had a drink, enough appetizers, ice, and napkins? They clearly were not enjoying themselves. Of course you have. Maybe you're even that hostess; and if so, stop it, and enjoy your company. That's what I do. Whenever we had company, after everyone left, Danny would say, "You are the worst hostess."

To which I would reply, "Thank you." He never said it in a mean way. He would say it because I don't wait on my company nonstop, frantically running from person to person and filling glasses before they're empty. After I take their coats (if need be) and get them their first beverage of choice, they're on their own. I sit among my family and friends and simply enjoy them. They know where refills are.

Why have company if all you're trying to do is be the best hostess? Do you really need people to say, "She's the best hostess?" I like being the "worst" hostess, as I always have a great time, even though apparently someone came close to dying of hunger and/or thirst. When you have people in your life that you think so much of that you invite them into your home to share good food and good company, enjoy them. Really enjoy them because there is no guarantee you will ever see them again. I know that sounds bleak, but it's true. Is it not?

All that to say, one evening we were sitting in his chair; and he said, "You know, honey. You may be the worst hostess, but you're the best caretaker."

I felt a smile well up in my heart and I looked up at him and said, "And which is better?"

He hugged me tight and said, "Caretaker, for sure."

For all your hard work today, I think you deserve a hug? Would you like that?

That is one of the four things he told me that will stay forever in my heart. The other three are as follows:

He told me he thanked God for me every day, which meant the world to me. This man that I love so much loves me so much that he thanks the God who created us for me.

He told me I was the best thing that ever happened to him. I feel the same way about him.

He told me I saved his life. He was referring to his years of drug addiction. During those difficult years, I recall one night when I was so distraught and tired of dealing with his addiction I was on my knees, crying so hard the tears weren't even hitting my face; they just fell to the floor. I expressed to God that I knew he didn't want me to leave him. In fact, the thought of leaving him hurt me to the core, so he needed to give me a love for this man that I never had. He did just that. I believe God, through me, actually saved his life. God honored my plea and gave me a love for this man that I treasured. I will always keep these four very touching, very profound truths in my heart.

The Truth, the Whole Truth, and Nothing But the Truth

Danny didn't say things he didn't mean just to say them. Here's one I will never forget because it was the one time I wished he hadn't been so honest. I'm all about honesty, but well judge for yourself.

We had been dating for quite some time when, after an intimate moment, I told him I loved him for the first time. It was a realization that just came over me. I remember feeling so contented to be there in his arms, my head resting on his chest, feeling, for the first time in a long time, in love. Suddenly I had no inhibition about sharing this with him, so I did. His reply, "Thank you." Whoa! Did he just thank me?

The sound of a stereo needle screeching across vinyl went through my brain! Luckily, he couldn't see, but my eyes flew open. I felt my stomach and my face twist at the same time. And oh my gosh if there was ever a time when I wished there was a rewind button for life, this was it! I truly didn't say it because I wanted him to say it back to me, but I was so sure we were on the same page at this point in our relationship. Clearly, I was way off…but was I?

Approximately one month later, he told me he loved me and explained how at that time I said it he just wasn't there yet, and he didn't want to say it just to say it. My, how thoughtful of him. For goodness sake, he was almost there, just a few weeks out. How could he not know that?

Countless Blessings

Over these past two years, I cannot list all the blessings that were bestowed upon us. So many people stepped up to help us in so many ways. Family and friends alike, which includes our church family and my work family. So many dinners were cooked and food service gift cards given. One dear friend sent her landscaper over to clean up our yard, and that same friend hired someone to wash our windows. The monetary gifts seem to come just when I wasn't sure how I was going to pay our taxes. There were collections taken at work.

The first one was taken so that I could stay overnight in the city the first night after his surgery and then go in each day during that week in May of 2018 when he had his kidney removed. The second collection was taken so that I could bring in extra help as Danny began to decline. I couldn't believe how much was collected and I was reduced to tears with gratitude and humility. I wish I could list every person, but I would fear leaving someone out. No matter, God knows who they are, and may he bless them all tenfold for their generous hearts. Their compassion let me know I'm not alone either.

These many acts of kindness aided us along. That said, there is always someone who is just mean. Why? I think so that we appreciate the kindhearted people. No need to go into detail but suffice it to say I focused on them for longer than I should have. If you come upon someone who is toxic, especially when you're going through a trial, pay them no mind. I cannot emphasize this enough; and while this may be difficult to do, you must, for your own self-preservation. As the adage says, "count your blessings not your troubles."

I believe God placed this on my heart, when the thought came to me, and it really woke me up. It was as if he was saying you have many wonderful people in your life, more than most, and to focus on the one or two who are mean is doing a great disservice to those who love you and continue to do so much for you. I'm grateful the malcontents in my world are few.

The Difficult Choice

As Danny continued to decline, I slept on the sofa, as I needed to be near him. He was now on hospice care and we had a hospital bed in our living room. The slightest movement made me jump to my feet. I had a discussion with the hospice nurse about getting a catheter, but he begged me not to, so I didn't. Not the right choice.

One Friday morning my friend Kathy called to say she would be over around noon. Danny had gotten much worse, so I wasn't sure he would even know who she was. And they were very close friends (she lives in North Haledon, New Jersey, about forty minutes north of us, so we don't get to see each other as much as we'd like). While she was here, we were in the kitchen and I heard movement coming from the living room. I ran in to find him out of bed and needing to use the bathroom. He was so unsteady, and I was fearful he would fall. I tried to get him to use the commode, but he became very angry, refusing to. He was loud and combative, which was so out of character for him.

Kathy came running in and was able to calm him down. She told me to call hospice and tell them we needed a nurse here immediately to insert a catheter. They said they would have someone here as soon as possible; and a few hours later, an angel showed up at our door. The minute I saw her, before even letting her in, I knew she was sent from God. She had a lovely, serene way about her. Her face was almost radiant and calming. I brought her over to Danny to explain why she was here. Initially he was having none of it, yelling to the point that I was looking on with horror, and Kathy told me to go to the kitchen. I ran outside to the backyard in tears, and I sat out on the patio until the yelling stopped. She was so good with Danny, explaining everything to him in the gentlest way. This was what Kathy told me and I was comforted by this. Having that catheter made all the difference in the world. I still slept on the sofa, but I no longer jumped at every little move he made. I was able to sleep more soundly and so was he.

I thought that by complying with his request to not get a catheter, I was being the caretaker he needed. Sometimes being the best caretaker means making the hard, but necessary decisions. It was no coincidence that Kathy, who cared for her terminally ill mom a few years back, was there to help me in ways that I didn't even know I needed the help. Another cherished friend.

Planning Arrangements

About ten years into our marriage, we had our wills drawn up and decided on what funeral home we would use. We also decided we both wanted to be cremated...so compatible. It just so happened our friend and neighbor, Jon, now worked as a mortician at the funeral home we chose. It's so surreal to even be writing this. He mentioned to me that it would be best if I didn't wait until Danny passed to make the arrangements. So I took his advice and called the funeral director.

Generally, funeral directors don't make house calls; but I couldn't leave Danny, so he offered to come to our home (having Jon as a friend helped, no doubt). Not knowing what to expect, I called my sister. I wanted her to be with me, because I was nervous about this. Unfortunately, she and my brother-in-law were in Virginia helping my niece, Marissa, move into her new apartment. I then called a friend who was out of work; but unbeknownst to me, she started a new job that day. I panicked, feeling so alone. Then God reminded me I was not alone. He knows what I need more than anyone; and when I met this gentleman, my fears immediately subsided. And he walked me through the process and was so compassionate.

Once we went over everything, I told him that Danny's siblings would be over later, and I wanted them to know exactly what was going on and to be able to talk about any concerns they might have. He said he would come back, and he did. This man was meant for this job. He was everything you would want in a funeral director, even though you have no idea what that is.

Thankfully Danny slept through both visits, which was a blessing because I don't know how I would have introduced them. I ponder this. "Honey, this is Matthew…he's uh, hmm."

So a day or so after that, my brother-in-law, Ray, came by to hang out with Danny while I ran some errands. He didn't know Danny slept through all the funeral arrangements, so he mentions it to him. Yeah, really. Of all the subjects to bring up! So when I came home, he pulled me aside and told me he mentioned to Danny that he heard the funeral arrangements were made. Clearly I do not have enough challenges in my life. Oh boy, I wasn't mad at him, not at all. I just wasn't sure what to expect. After he left, I'm sitting with Danny; and he asked, "Did you make arrangements for my funeral?" I took a deep breath and looked my baby straight in his eyes and said, ever so slowly, nodding my head, "Yes, honey. I did."

He looked at me and simply said, "That's good."

And then he put his arms around me as if to say, "I know that couldn't have been easy."

July 25, 2019

Today Ray came over so that I could get my nails done. My niece, Marissa, is getting married on Saturday, July 27, and I planned on getting my nails done and a spray tan. Danny and I had discussed this. He so wanted to attend her wedding; but at the time we talked about it, we weren't sure if he'd be able to. He was fine with me going. So I got my nails done and was going to leave at around 6:30 PM for the spray tan. Don't judge me, I was pasty.

Danny's brother, Ron, and sister, Carolyn, were at the house as were our friends, Fran and Jon, who live directly across the street. Danny had a special relationship with Fran, as their schedules provided many opportunities to chat as they were going to and coming home from work. It was nearing time for me to go; and as we all stood around his bed, I confirmed they were okay with me leaving for a short while and said I'd be back soon. With that, I went upstairs to get my things. Suddenly, I heard Fran calling me. I was standing at the top of the stairs looking down at her; and she looked up at me and simply said, "He's gone." I dropped my bag and ran downstairs. His brother and sister came into the living room from the dining room, and we watched him take a breath or two more. And then he was gone. The hospice nurse said he would most likely leave us when he was sure I wasn't around. He thought I had left.

I just stared at him and without thought I brushed my hand over his eyes, barely touching them to close them. I had no way of knowing this moment would come when it did, even though I knew it was coming. All I could think as I looked down at him was, "I will no longer be able to kiss your forehead or place my head to your temples with my hand upon your cheek and feel your hand on my arm, gently squeezing it." I thought I had more time, not much more, but a little more.

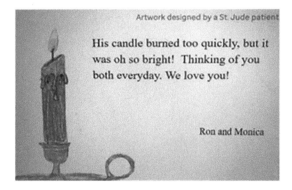

Artwork designed by a St. Jude patient

His candle burned too quickly, but it was oh so bright! Thinking of you both everyday. We love you!

Ron and Monica

This was the last Bitmoji from my Danny...it took my breath away.

I'm always with you

Another Choice

In case you're wondering if I went to Marissa's wedding, I did. I have been close to her since the day she was born. When she was a little girl, we took walks together almost every Saturday during the warmer months. She was a fun and funny little girl who grew up to be a beautiful and funny young woman. Was it difficult? That would be a resounding *yes*. But it wasn't about me nor was it about Danny. It was about Marissa and Grayson. Did I have a good time? I did. I was surrounded by family and friends who didn't judge me but understood my thought process, which simply put, it wasn't about me. Did I ever get the spray tan? No. Priorities change. It no longer bothered me that I was pasty.

The one thing that made going to the wedding bearable was not turning around as I left the house and seeing my sweet man lying in that hospital bed. That was always one of the most difficult things I've ever had to do, and I had done it often. My cousin Larry; his wife, Lynel; daughter, Leanne; and her husband, James, picked me up so I wouldn't have to go alone. That was a blessing…my emotions were all over the radar. I felt numb.

More meanness has reared its ugly head, in that I was judged for really petty things. Was I hurt? Yes, I was. My husband just passed, and I'm feeling disoriented and drained. But because of the person who judged me, it didn't come as a big shock. Again, when dealing with toxic people, you must let it roll off your back. Is it easy? No. But it is so important, especially when you are feeling fragile. Please, try to remember this fact; *nobody* but God is your judge. *Romans 8:31, NIV* reads, "If God is for us, who can be against us?"

Farewell: July 28, 2020

The day of Danny's funeral is somewhat of a blur. What I do remember is arriving an hour before visitation hours began. It was me and his entire family, and we were taken into a room where he was laid out in a cremation casket. Since neither of us wanted to be on display, and since he was being cremated, he was kept in a private room for just immediate family to come and say our goodbyes.

There he was, my love, seemingly asleep and I just broke down. Thankfully Ron was standing next to me and placed his arm around my shoulders. Everyone was crying. I can't begin to imagine the pain felt by his mom.

The hour seemed to go by quickly and then the guests started to arrive. There was a constant flow of visitors coming through. I also remember standing by myself, which I regret, because I don't know why I stood alone. It was definitely not a conscience decision, and it bears no significance. But I wish I had stood with his mom.

I think to myself, "I know I'll see him again, but he won't be wearing the cute golf outfit I put together for him." I remember when I brought the outfit to the funeral home, as Jon requested, I made sure the pale yellow golf shirt had no stains; and much to my amazement, it didn't. However, I didn't think to check his khakis; and when I unfolded them in front of Jon, there was a stain, of course. I was hard-pressed to find an article of clothing of Danny's without a stain. I suppose it's his signature. I'm certain he'd agree.

A Friend in Need

It was a Saturday and I needed someone to talk to. I could feel it brimming within me and I couldn't get a grip. I called Fran and she said to come over. The minute I saw her, the tears began to flow. We went out on her back porch. The second we sat down, I literally cried on her shoulder for some time. She just let me cry and I will forever be grateful for that. She didn't have to say a word. I just needed her shoulder and she lent it to me.

My New Beginning

From time to time, Danny would ask me if I was going to be okay. I told him, not at first. That much I knew. I said it will take a while; but I'm sure, eventually I'll be okay. I had no idea how difficult adjusting to this new chapter of my life would be; and it doesn't get easier, not yet anyway. In fact, it seems to get tougher. I miss him desperately and I always will. I feel like I'm floundering. Strange thought, I also realize I need to be careful when flying down the stairs or cooking (or attempting to cook anyway). My man isn't here in case I get hurt, nor will he be here when I come down with a bad cold or flu. I try not to dwell on these thoughts, as it won't do me any good.

Some time has passed; I'm getting on pretty well. Mornings are relatively easy because throughout our marriage, our mornings were busy getting ready for work. The evenings, ugh. For the first three months after he passed, I would come home and sit on the sofa, facing his favorite chair, and cry. It was physically painful to come home, knowing his absence would tear at my heart. I had no idea how long this would go on. It's not like I had much control over it, my heart was broken, and I couldn't help that. Then something happened.

Mold Happened

I discovered I have mold in the basement. Yup, but it ended my evening ritual of coming home and bawling my eyes out. How? Well when I discovered there was mold in the basement, I knew I had to act quickly. So first things first, I asked my neighbors, Jon and Kalman, to help me clear out the basement...no small task. I had already given some good furniture to someone who needed it. The rest is not saleable. So every Monday night, they would come over and haul everything from entertainment centers (we had two) to a sofa and chaise and a big old chest, just to name a few. It was a standing date for some time, as we are only allowed three big items each week. I am thankful for bulk trash Tuesdays and for Jon and Kalman. I'm forever grateful for all they did.

Then my friend Karen told me her husband was a contractor and he would be willing to come by and see how bad it was. He, Andy, came over and confirmed that the mold was along the bottom of the wall only and that he could remedy it. So he and Dean, his colleague, got to work. They were in my basement for approximately three months…lots of issues. So every night when I came home, the minute I walked in the door, I would hear, "Kathy's home! How was your day? Come, see what we've done!" This always made me laugh and ended my tearful conversations with the vacant chair. God is so good. He always manages to take the not-so-good stuff in our lives, like mold, and turn it into something good.

November 28, 2019: Thanksgiving

My first Thanksgiving driving by myself to Danny's sister's, Carolyn's, house. This was so difficult. No Danny to play radio games or tell to slow down or play with his earlobe (yes, the secret is out, I had a thing for his earlobes). But I wasn't alone. My nieces and nephew lost their Uncle Danny. His sister lost her brother. Kathy and Chuck lost a beloved friend; and their daughters, Brianna and Jenna, lost their beloved "uncle." Saddest of all, my mother-in-law, Irene, lost her child, her Danny, and my heart breaks for her still.

November 29, 2019

It's the day after Thanksgiving. My plan was to put up the Christmas tree. First, I decided to watch the last episode of *Survivor* that I recorded. The show ends and out of nowhere the tears start flowing. Missing him just seems too much to bear, but I press on. I think about the tree again and it feels like an overwhelming task. The thought of doing this pulls at my hurting heart. The thought of not doing it feels even worse. Suddenly I feel God's peace envelope me and I smile through my tears and I thank Him. He is with me and he, above everyone, understands.

Interjected Thought #2: Think Before You Say

One of the responses that I find off-putting is when someone tells me they know how I feel because they lost a parent. You can't possibly know how someone who lost the love of their life feels, because you lost a parent. I lost both of my parents and I miss them to this day. But losing my Danny does not compare. I would never tell a parent who lost a child I know how they feel. I have no doubt this is said to make someone like me feel like I'm not alone in my loss. But in reality, it feels more like it's minimizing my loss.

Christmas Eve 2019

It's Christmas Eve. Danny and I hosted his family every year since his parents moved into the Piscataway Senior Citizen Center. We always have a great time. This year I looked forward to all of us being together, as we were all hurting, and I felt being together would aid in our healing. Ron had put together a video, memories of Danny; and he asked me if I would be up for seeing it. I was. I sat between my nieces and we held hands as we watched. We laughed, we cried, and we were united in our heartache.

Christmas Day 2019

Today marks five months since Danny passed. I went to Marylou and Ray's, as they always host Christmas Day. I love being with my family. It's always a treat to see Marissa and Grayson, who you can always count on for entertaining stories. There was laughter, and I had a good time, but I couldn't ignore the void in my heart. It helped that my ninety-three-year-old aunt and her ninety-eight-year-old boyfriend (yeah, really) joined us this year. He talks really loudly, but he doesn't know it. So he was confounded as to how we could hear things he was muttering to my aunt. Thankfully he was just telling her things like what he was going to eat next…whew!

December 31, 2019

Oh boy, New Year's Eve. We always celebrated with our neighborhood family at Jon and Fran's house across the street. They asked if I would be coming and there was no place else I wanted to be. Some people who have gone through what I'm going through choose to do something different and I understand that. It's a personal choice. I love my friends…they're family, and I wanted to be with them. When it was time for the ball to drop, I had no idea how this would play out. Would I be standing alone; and if so, well it would only be for a few seconds…oh the thought. Well, when the ball was about to drop, my dear sweet, ever so thoughtful friends gathered around me, Gabbie, Kalman, Fran, Jon, Ileana, and Joe, and we did one big group hug. And I was beyond grateful for this. They made ringing in the new year more than bearable. They shed a soft, warm glowing light on my life; and while I know the road ahead will still be rough, these friends of mine are so precious to me.

January 10, 2020

Today is the Friday before my arthroscopic knee surgery, which is this coming Wednesday, January 15. I came home from work and it occurred to me that this is another first without Danny. I began to cry and this one was uncontrollable. I texted my friend, Estrella, and she texted back that she was on a business call. I texted back, "No problem," but she sensed something wasn't right. She called shortly thereafter and told me to come over. Before I could get my coat on, there she was at my door. We hugged and then walked back to her house. We had dinner with her husband, George, and son, Stephen. I was there until 1:30 in the morning (we never run out of things to talk about, it's uncanny). I felt so much better.

Two Days Later: January 12, 2020—Scratch That

This was a very difficult weekend for me, for no particular reason. I was very emotional and cried, a lot. Case in point, Friday night. That said, over the past several weeks when doing laundry, I would venture into the room in the basement where we had the pool table. I'm terrible at pool, but like bowling, which I am equally terrible at, I like playing. Time and again I'd scratch early in the game, two balls in and scratch. I never got past three balls in before scratching.

So there I am staring at the pool table. I think to myself, "Aren't you feeling bad enough?" Apparently not, although my emotions would beg to differ. What was it that compelled me to want to do this again, when I was feeling so sad? Did I feel that I had improved from the last bad game? No. Did I suddenly feel empowered? Not even a little bit. Still, I picked up the pool stick, looked up, and said to the drop ceiling, in an authoritative tone, "Show me how it's done!" I then took a deep breath and played the best game of pool ever. Okay, so the bar wasn't raised all that high. But I was getting each ball in without scratching, and I don't think I exhaled until it was over. I almost took a bow. I lay down the stick and walked away. My heart was feeling a little lighter...I really needed that. I never played another game. A few months later, I sold the pool table to someone who appreciated it and was no doubt a much better pool player.

January 15, 2020

Going in for arthroscopic knee surgery due to a torn meniscus. My brother-in-law, Ray, is bringing me. I so appreciate this, but it causes me to miss Danny so much. Always being there for each other, especially at times like this, was something I suppose I took for granted. As the only song I ever liked by Joni Mitchell says, "Don't it always seem to go, you don't know what you've got till it's gone."

My surgeon had met Danny before, so when he asked me if I wanted him to call home, I just stared at him and said "no, that's ok."

He said it would be no problem, but I couldn't get the words out. So I thanked him, but said no, that's ok. I felt like a parrot. I was afraid if I said more, I would break down in tears.

January 18, 2020

Several months ago I was looking through Danny's clothes, not in a hurry to part with them. This is also a process. As I look through his T-shirts, I don't know what to do. I think T-shirts tell a bit about the personality of a person.

How could I part with these? I mention it to my friend, Fran, and she suggested I have a quilt made. Oh my gosh, I thought this is a brilliant idea, so I did just that. I found them on Etsy, Project Repat. They made it so easy and I was so excited.

It came in the mail today. You know what else came today? Our first snowfall! Coincidence? I think not.

January 23, 2020

I walked into the bedroom, and I noticed one of his ties poking out from inside the closet door where his tie rack hung. I walked over to fix it and I stood there staring at his ties. I reflect back to the many mornings he'd be getting dressed, while I was in the bathroom putting on makeup; and he would inevitably say, "Hey, babe. Would you come here a minute and pick out a tie?" His questions varied depending on what he was wearing, but he valued my opinion, as he should. I have a good sense of style. I'm not bragging, just stating a fact. Ask any one of my friends.

As I write this, the memory makes me smile. Once we decided on his outfit, I would tell him how handsome he looked, because he always looked so handsome whether he was in a suit or jeans and a t-shirt.

I had a follow-up visit with my orthopedic surgeon today. Afterward, I passed by Danny's favorite seafood restaurant in Westfield. We went there frequently; and George, the owner, and Danny had a friendly relationship. Danny thought the world of George. Months before, I had placed one of the memorial cards from Danny's service in an envelope with a note to George, but there never seemed to be an appropriate time to drop it off.

It was around 10:30 AM. So I pulled over, figuring I'd drop off the envelope to whoever was there, and they would give it to George. I didn't expect him to be there, but he was. I didn't know if he'd heard of Danny's passing; and when I walked in and saw him, I became so emotional. I could hardly speak. I managed to tell him Danny had passed away, and the look of sadness that came over him was more than I could bear. I just handed him the envelope; and in barely a whisper I said, "Danny thought the world of you, George," and motioned toward the door that I had to go. I cried all the way home.

Later that day I was talking with my friend, Lori, telling her how there are times when I still can't believe he's gone. She said, "I know. It just doesn't seem right." It was that simple. So many had gone in our lives; but this, the passing of my Danny was somehow bewildering. She was also very close with Danny; in fact, it was Lori who fixed me up on a blind date with him. Funny story, but you'll have to wait.

February 2, 2020

Today is Super Bowl Sunday. SBS was Danny's party. He really did it up, grilling New York Strip Steaks, twice-baked potatoes, great apps (actually I made the apps). He so enjoyed everything SBS, especially having his mom, his sister, and our nieces over. Another painful first and with all the hype on TV, there was no avoiding it. Sadly, I didn't even entertain the thought of hosting. It just didn't feel right. The void was too big; and I couldn't even bring up the subject to his family, knowing they too, were hurting.

First thing in the morning, I went to church then I visited Danny's cousin, Elaine, who is battling cancer. I liked Elaine the instant I met her. She's kind and genuine. I enjoy her and her family. We had a delicious brunch of homemade waffles, compliments of her husband, Vinnie, and I was thankful she was up for the visit.

On the way home, I tried not to think about the game. I ran a couple of errands. And on my way to get gas, the flood gates opened, and I couldn't stop the tears from coming. Living in New Jersey, we don't pump our own gas, so I wondered, as I pulled into the gas station, what the attendant might be thinking? I didn't care. Disturbingly enough, he didn't seem to care either.

Once home, after about an hour, I settled down and bravely turned on the game. I don't even like football; but for some strange reason, I felt compelled to watch or at least have it on to catch the commercials. It turned out to be a pretty good game and the commercials weren't half bad either.

Interjected Thought #3: Good Grief

Before you ask someone who has lost a loved one about grief counseling, feel them out first. I say this because when someone asks me how I'm doing and I tell them I miss Danny, but I do feel God is healing my heart more each day, they inevitably say, "Have you tried grief counseling?" Or they'll give me the name of a grief counseling group. It's as if my sadness or grief, if you will, isn't "normal" after a certain time, and being asked that question makes me feel as though my grieving after only eight months now requires that I seek help in the way of group counseling sessions.

I'm sure grief counseling helps a lot of people. I'm also sure those who suggest this have sincere intentions, but grief counseling is not a one-size-fits-all solution. For me, the thought of sitting with a group of people talking about how much I miss my husband and listening to them tell me how much they miss their loved ones doesn't appeal to me. That said, my church offered a one-day grief seminar before Christmas that I found to be a perfect fit for me. It was designed to help us face the holidays and it was just what I needed. I found it beneficial as my first Christmas without Danny was upon me.

Grief is a process and I go with it; I think that's healthy. Throughout my grief God has given me his priceless gift of peace. It is truly a peace that surpasses all understanding.

I recently read this, and it resonated with me, "Those who think there is a time limit when grieving have never lost a piece of their heart."

I've been told that one of the stages of grief is anger. I have not felt angry, not at all. In the book of John Chapter 16 verse 33, Jesus said "I have told you these things so that in me you may have peace. In this world you will have trouble. But take heart! I have overcome the world." I do take heart.

The intensity that I miss Danny will never lessen. But the sadness and grief will, of this I have no doubt.

February 9, 2020: A Look Back on The Blind Date to End All Blind Dates (28 Years Ago Today)

I don't make New Year's resolutions. I believe if you want to start something or end something, do it when you think of it. Why wait? However, it was January of 1992; and while driving home one night, belting out Queen's "Somebody to Love," I resolved to go out on a date with anyone (well almost anyone) that someone wanted to set me up with.

Lori took me up on it. Ugh, me and my big mouth. We were both in wholesale window treatment sales, and one day she's in a client's carpet store as is Danny (he sold carpet wholesale and was setting up a display for the client). He ordered pizza for the three of them, which gave Lori time to get to know him a little. When he left, she thought, "I wonder if he's single." So she ran after him and asked if he was dating anyone; and when he said no, she told him about me. He asked if I was as pretty as her and she told him I was really nice.

You can imagine my delight when she told me this! I felt like I had just won Miss Congeniality in a beauty pageant! I asked her why she said that; and she said she felt it was a shallow question and if he didn't call, he wasn't worth it. Well, I had to admit she had a point (my girlfriend always looking out for me); to his credit, he called. I found him easy to talk with; so I had to admit, I was a little excited. However, the stress of anticipating another bad date prompted me to tell her, "This is the last blind date I'm going on!" Hmmm, prophetic?

I was so sure this was going to be a waste of time, so I didn't go crazy getting ready. In fact, quite the opposite. I went for a five-mile run, then to Dunkin Donuts for coffee, and then down to my mom's to celebrate my sister's, Judy's, birthday. It was *February 9, 1992*; her actual birthday is the 10th, but we celebrated on the Sunday. I made the date for a Sunday so that I could use the "I have to get up early for work excuse," if it's going badly. While at my mom's, my sister, Marylou, told me my hair looked really good, so I thought, "Great, one less thing to deal with." My "date" was coming at 6:00 PM so I left my mom's at 5:15ish. My mom lived approximately twenty minutes away (just to give you an idea about how thrilled I was to be going on this date). Once home, I washed under my arms and threw on my favorite jeans and brushed my…teeth. Ah, you thought I was going to say my hair, didn't you? I was ready.

He arrived on time, and when I opened the door, I was pleasantly surprised. He was tall and very handsome, what a relief! The last guy Lori wanted to fix me up with looked like he was in the process of morphing from ape to man! He was really hairy. It was summertime, we were at a picnic, and he had a tank top on. Enough said.

Within the first five minutes, I discovered that we had met five years earlier when he was selling carpet on the retail end. You see, when he walked into my apartment, he commented on how nice the carpet was for a rental. I told him I bought it, that it didn't come with the apartment. He asked where and when I told him he said he used to manage that store. All of a sudden, I realized he was the handsome salesman; and just like in the movies, I had a flashback! I'll explain.

Five years earlier, I had just moved into my apartment in an old Victorian house in Madison, New Jersey, and was buying carpet. He happened to be the manager of the store; and when I first saw him, I commented to my sister how handsome he was. Her comment: "Yeah, but he's a salesman." I knew what she meant, but I was in sales too, so not every salesperson is shady. Anyway, turned out, I made a mistake when ordering my carpet, as I had a vision that didn't work out the way I had hoped. And when I called to see if it could be rectified, he did me the favor. He actually recalled that incident and said he had no idea what made him want to help me. With the mistake I made, he said he normally would not have been able to do what he did for me, which was to get me another piece and try to match the dye lot, which I told him wasn't necessary because most of it would be covered by furniture. He said he never did anything like that again.

I once asked him if had I been in the carpet store instead of Lori, would he have asked me out. He said no. He said he would have never assumed I would want to go out with him. I loved his humility.

February 14, 2020

We never made too big a deal on Valentine's Day, but this year I received so many thoughtful gifts from unexpected people, one whom I have never met. Many thanks to Chris, Rob, Marylou, and Sarah. You all made me feel so special and so loved.

This was my last Valentine Bitmoji from Danny last year, still sporting his Jamaican tan.

March 5, 2020: My Birthday

Another first…my birthday. It's the first time in twenty-five years that I didn't hear "Happy birthday baby," first thing in the morning. I did manage to get up and teach my "Just Pump It" class. I teach spin and weight/cardio classes at the YMCA (I may have mentioned that). Afterward, I had my coffee, showered, and headed down to Ocean Grove to meet my girlfriends, Deonna and Lori; and off we went to the Philadelphia Flower Show. We've been going to this show for years. It was a beautiful day, warm, and sunny. Later we enjoyed dinner at The Love. All in all a great day and I thank God for my girlfriends.

March 11–15, 2020: Heading to North Carolina

At this point in time we're just hearing about the coronavirus. It was known about in China, but not yet in the USA. I was leaving for North Carolina on the 12th to spend a mostly girls' weekend with my sister-in-law, Monica, and my niece, Veronica. The minute I saw Monica at the airport, I knew this would be a great visit and it was.

We got to the house and it was so good to see Ron. It was nice to relax and catch up. Monica and I never run out of things to talk about, and so we were getting caught up while waiting for Veronica. She has a long drive from Winston-Salem. I'm looking forward to seeing her sweet, beautiful face! Then it's off to dinner.

Dinner started out great, we were looking over the menu options, also deciding on wine, and all the while I'm feeling so happy to be there with them. Our waiter starts out nice enough, but it didn't take long before I got the feeling this guy's life could turn into a Lifetime movie (very different from a Hallmark movie). We learned how old he is—I think we were supposed to be shocked by his "youthful" appearance—how he hates his ex-wife; and how he's engaged to a woman who doesn't speak English…wait until she finds out what she said yes to. He also managed to insult all of us regarding our politics. And when it comes to politics, that's where we differ, so that he managed to insult all of us was quite something. Strange dude.

I was introduced to disc golf, which I thoroughly enjoyed, and I wasn't as awful as I thought I would be. It was all of us: Ron; Monica; Veronica; her husband, Josh; and Zorro, the cutest, most lovable pup.

Our time together was so special. We did a lot, yet it wasn't rushed. We went to an art showing (someday Veronica will be showing, as she is an amazing artist), to a beautiful arboretum, and the North Carolina Museum of Art where I saw a sculpture that reminded me of a picture of Danny that Monica took a few years ago. When I mentioned this to her, she knew the photo I was talking about. We also had some touching moments. I am so comfortable being here with them, appreciating life. As my visit begins to wind down, COVID-19 seems to be ramping up. Had I had my laptop with me, I wouldn't have minded staying, because at this point, I just found out we were told to work from home. It really didn't matter whose home!

Life imitating art

March 25, 2020

It's eight months since Danny's passing. The most unsettling thing happened this morning and it upset me the entire day. I was sound asleep and from what I could determine I wasn't dreaming. Suddenly, in a loud, audible voice I heard, "Hey, Kath?" It was clearly Danny's voice and I bolted upright in bed, my heart pounding so hard it felt like it was going to burst from my chest. I sat there waiting, for what I didn't know. I whispered, "Dan?" Then I began to cry.

It's 9:30 PM; I'm still feeling rattled. I know Danny is in heaven and I know that was not him. There are some, well-intentioned people who would say he was reaching out to me. But I know that's not true. Similar things like that have happened to me in the past. I'd be sound asleep and be jolted because I thought I heard a door slam. That was nothing compared to how shaken this made me.

I'm using a journal to write down all my notes for this story. It was given to me by my friend, Karen, and each page has scripture verses. On the pages of notes that I write about this unnerving incident of hearing Danny's voice is scripture from Psalm 25:4–5 and Philippians 4:7 and I am comforted.

The Question of Journaling

Speaking of journals, I've never been into journaling. I am happy to have this journal, as it has come at the perfect time. It has kept me from scrambling for paper every time I want to add to my story. However, journaling isn't my thing. Over the years I have been given many journals, and I've either given them away or used the pages to make shopping lists. People who journal would ask if I journal and my response: "No, it's not my thing." They would look at me with a puzzled look and ask, "Well, have you given it a try?" Again, I would say, "No, I know it's not my thing." This confounds the journaling sect.

I get it though. I feel that same enthusiasm about online banking. I am baffled at folks who don't bank online.

The Poem

A couple of months ago, I was looking for something, when I came upon a poem Danny had written to me about ten years into our marriage. When he originally gave it to me, he had his mom write it out in calligraphy. I had never seen his original handwritten version. I had it framed; but when we had our bedroom painted, I put it away and forgot about it. What I found was his handwritten version. I felt my heart laugh with joy, as I was thrilled to have this, and I didn't waste any time buying a frame for it. It's the only poem he'd ever written to me; that's what makes it so special.

Although the footprints I make
May leave only one set
I've never felt alone
Not since the first day we met
We'll have our disagreements
And maybe sometimes we'll fight
But I know you'll be next to me
As I sleep every night.
You're so very special to me
I don't think that you know.
That's why I truly believe
Our love will continue to grow
Many things have helped me
To learn the true meaning of life
The most important of which
Is having you for my wife
I'll be there for you always
From now till the end
It's such a warm comfortable feeling
To know you're my best friend.

All my love.

Danny

The Things That Haunt Me

Initially, after he passed, I kept thinking of the times when he had really declined and the look in his eyes that told me he was so tired of fighting this battle. I would always kiss him on the forehead, my palm to his sweet face to let him know how much I love him. His eyes would soften, and my heart would melt.

Suffering isn't just about pain. Danny suffered in many ways and I did all I could to let him know he wasn't alone *and he wasn't a burden.*

> ➤ It was a hot Saturday afternoon and we had lost power. Jon, our neighbor, called to tell me that he had to run out and

if the power didn't come back by the time he returned, he would start up our generator. Within the hour it came back on and Danny had fallen asleep. The sun was setting; so as not to wake him, I kept the lights off as well as the TV and I went upstairs to read, leaving our bedroom door ajar and the air conditioning on low in case he called for me. About fifty minutes went by, so I went down to check on him, and there he was sitting up looking terrified. I had never seen him look like this; and when he saw me, he started bawling, telling me he thought I had been killed and why didn't I answer him when he was screaming for me. I ran over to him and checked him all over to make sure he wasn't hurt, and I wrapped my arms around him and told him I didn't hear him and that I was so sorry and to please forgive me. He sat there and wouldn't look at me, and I kept kissing the top of his head, arms still around him. And he finally said he forgave me, but not to ever do that again. He was like a little boy. Of course, I have no doubt that the meds had everything to do with this, coupled with the fact that he woke up and it was dark and quiet. But this haunted me for weeks, months even, as I wondered how long he was thinking, fearing that I had been killed. Ugh, just recalling this incident is distressing.

➤ When he realized he no longer had control over his body, he sobbed uncontrollably into my neck, "I can't do this, honey."

I said, "Baby, you are not alone. I am here with you, and I will take good care of you." But the pain and sadness struck at the very core of my being; and I hugged him so tight, kissing his face and not knowing what to say. There are no words, but there is love and compassion. And that is what I gave, and I gave him my all. There is the knowing that this beautiful gift of love we have says, without words, "I will stay here with you, and I will not move except to hug you and caress your back, our heads gently touching, for as long as you need me to." My arms may become tired, and my legs may cramp, but I will not move. I don't know how long we stayed in that embrace. The tears spilling from our eyes seemed endless, as we held onto each other just as we'd done so many times before, neither of us wanting to let go.

➤ Eventually his wrist and hands became weak and it was difficult for him to hold things. I brought him a protein shake and I shook it up for him and removed the cap. I handed it to him; and out of habit he shook it, not realizing the cap was off. And chocolate went everywhere! My eyes widened as we looked at each other; and I quickly went over, caught the drink, and told him, "Baby, I will have you cleaned up in no time. Don't you worry." He kept apologizing and I kept telling him not to worry. After I put clean clothes on him and clean sheets, I wiped up the rest of the chocolate. All clean I sat down next to him to help him drink the shake; and he took my hand and patted it and said, "Honey, you really handled that quite well." I laughed; he looked adorable as he said this. His eyes held so much expression and I said, "I did, didn't I?" I'm smiling as I write this because it was a tender moment that felt so special.

I'm reading a book entitled *I Choose Peace* by *Doug Bender*. In it Kathie Lee Gifford writes regarding the many things God will do for those of us who trust him. She says, "He's going to help you forget the things that haunt you." How timely.

Interjected Thought #4: "Grant that I may not so much seek to be consoled, as to console."

When family and friends who hadn't seen Danny in a long time wanted to visit, I would forewarn them, just so they would be somewhat prepared, that he had lost a lot of weight and was frail. But I came to find that no amount of preparation helped; and each time they were overcome with sadness at seeing this once strong, vibrant, man reduced by the ravages of cancer. So we would go into the kitchen where he couldn't see how distraught they were, and I would hug them and comfort them as best I could. After all, they love him too.

Reflecting on Those Who Made This Journey Before Me

One of the many things this journey has uncovered for me is a lookback on those who went before me and the loves they left behind. My very first thought was my grandma, my mom's mom. My grandpa died at a pretty young age. He was a fun, life loving man who cherished his wife and family. I was five years old; and I remember when she got the news, I was there. And I remember how terribly distraught she was. But not until my Danny passed away would I ever be able to understand the magnitude of her grief.

My dad, Anthony Prillo. Ah, my hero. Everybody loved my dad, but no one as much as my mom. He was a very funny man, great with one-liners. We now fondly refer to them as tonyisms. I remember getting ready to go to the hospital to see him; and as I was leaving, my sister called to tell me he had passed away. My first thought was of my mom. I now had to deliver this news to her. The man she adored and who adored her for over fifty years is gone. I walked over to her house in a daze; and when I got to the front door, it was open. But the storm door was locked. I knocked. She walked to the door and before opening it she looked at me and said, "he's gone." It wasn't really a question. She just stood there for what seemed like forever and then opened the door, to her house and to her heart, and together we wept. My dad's death was the first time I ever truly grieved. I remember to this day, how my heart actually felt like it had broken. I never knew my heart could hurt more than it did that day. I know now.

My friend, Deonna, whose husband, Kurt, died tragically in a horrific accident just weeks after my dad had passed. They too had that something special. The news of what happened was shocking and it rocked her world to its core. How could it not. Her daughters were very young; and because she needed to be there for them, she was barely able to properly grieve.

My friend, Maureen, her husband, Gary, so genuine and fun. He loved life; he loved movies. He could imitate Kathy Bates with lines from the movie *Misery* and I would laugh every time. They, like us, did not have children, but they had that special connection that was felt more than seen.

Danny's cousin, Karen. She lost her husband, George, without warning, another unique union where you felt their mutual adoration for each other. He was a great guy who told it like it was. You knew where you stood with him. I appreciate people like that. I liked him the minute I met him.

Last, but certainly not least, my former landlady and forever friend, Fannie. She and her late husband, Gene, had that special something. Years before I met Danny, I knew I wanted what she and Gene had. They would come down to the old Victorian they owned that had three apartments in it. I lived in the middle one. While they would be taking care of whatever it was that needed tending to, they had this playful banter that was so much fun to watch. They didn't seem to realize what they were giving off. When he passed away, she was devastated and to this day she grieves his loss. He was a wonderful, loving husband. I make it a point to visit with her a couple of times a year. I love her as if she was my aunt, and I'm grateful she has nieces and nephews who love her and are there for her.

After their loves had passed, they carried on. Their hearts were broken, but they carried on. I, too, will carry on.

April 1, 2020

I had no intention of writing today, but I just received word that my pastor's son was killed in a car accident. I couldn't believe what I was hearing. It just doesn't seem plausible and all I can think about is Pastor Lloyd, his wife, Karen, and their family. What's worse, because of the *coronavirus* and the quarantine in place, I can't even show up at their door to bring comfort. I feel so helpless. Of course I'm praying for them, and I've reached out to others who I know will pray. But I can't help but reflect on the day after Danny passed away, they were on their way home from California. Once landing in Newark Airport, they came right over; and to this day, they will never know how much that meant to me. It was so heartening. They are both an amazing blessing in my life and not being able to be there for them is an awful feeling.

April 2nd: Sweet Dreams Are Made of This

I woke up recalling a dream about Danny. I dreamt I walked up to our bed and he was all comfy under the covers. I looked down at him and he looked up at me with his eyes smiling and I said, "You look so cozy." He said, "I am. Wanna join me?" I said, "Yeah, I do." That was it. It was enough to warm my heart and I'm thankful for the memory of this sweet, albeit, short dream.

April 4, 2020

Today we were all supposed to get together to spread Danny's ashes. It was me and as many members of his family who are able to be there. This date was suggested by Ron; since Danny's birthday is April 6th, we picked the closest Saturday. Unfortunately due to the coronavirus, we had to cancel our plans.

I also have plans to separate his ashes because our neighborhood family wants to be a part of spreading his ashes as well. I decided to divide this time between families simply because I feel it will be best for everyone. We have a date picked out with our neighborhood family, but that may be cancelled as well. We shall see.

April 6, 2020: Happy Birthday, My Love

Today is Danny's birthday, and first thing in the morning I began to cry. Man do I miss him. I posted a little "Happy birthday, my love" to him on Instagram, reflecting on each photo, and that brings a smile. But it was Candace and Casey who lifted my spirits in a text to me, recalling some things about their Uncle Danny that had me laughing. This was no small thing, because I know how much they miss him, and their hearts are hurting too. To be able to laugh is a gift. Laughter really is the best medicine and I so appreciated it. I'm ready to face the day, grateful for all that God has blessed me with.

April 10, 2020: Good Friday

I took a vacation day today, since I usually take Good Friday off. But since we're all still working from home, I needed a break from my laptop. I miss my boss, Tom. But in his thoughtfulness, he calls to make sure I'm okay, and I appreciate that. I miss my other work colleagues, as well. We really have a good team.

We were created to be together, not to be isolated. This causes me to contemplate those people who say they prefer animals to people, and I can't help but wonder if they still feel that way.

It being Good Friday, I took advantage of Sight & Sound running the *Jesus* play over this weekend only. It was originally supposed to run in the theaters, but the quarantine derailed that. It blew me away. It was so well done. And at the end I was bawling, which was the same reaction I had when I saw *The Passion of the Christ*. It's the only true story that I know the end, but it never ceases to reduce me to tears of humility. What Jesus Christ did for the entire human race, yesterday, today, and tomorrow, will always take my breath away.

After that I watched the Good Friday service online from my church. Pastor Lloyd delivered a wonderful message; and he did so during, what I can only imagine, the most difficult time he has ever faced in his life, the death of his son, Jeremy. My loss cannot compare. At the end of the service the song "It Is Well with My Soul" was played, and that song always puts a gigantic lump in my throat. But I am able to say, albeit, with difficulty, it is well with my soul.

April 12, 2020: Resurrection Sunday

I woke up this Easter Sunday feeling grateful to God for all he continues to do for me. Since COVID-19 is still at large, I'm not having the entire family over. But, thankfully, Marylou and Ray are coming over (we've spent a lot of time together over the past few weeks). It turned out to be a lovely day. I ordered food from The Garden Restaurant, which is owned by my friend Karen and her husband, and contractor, Andy. The food there never disappoints; not only that, it is exceptional. Marylou brought over some delicious fare and we had mimosas, which is the only way I'll drink orange juice or unless it's squeezed right from the orange.

When we were cleaning up the kitchen, Marylou pointed out that it was a much different Easter. The obvious difference, Danny was not here. But because of the virus, Judy, John, Marissa, Grayson, and Ray's friend, Mike, weren't here either. Somehow, that seemed to make Danny's absence more bearable, as there wasn't just one empty seat at the table; there were six empty seats.

After they left Gabbie texted to see if I was coming over to hang out in their driveway (we're observing the social distancing rules). I gladly went over; and it was me, Gabbie, Kalman, Jon, Fran, Michael,

Isabella, and Amelia. It was so nice talking, laughing, and just being with my other family.

Easter didn't begin or end as it had in years past; and I must admit, I was okay with that.

April 20, 2020: He'd Be Fishing

A thought occurred to me that even though we are all still quarantining and I'm working from home, I have not felt alone or lonely. I find this noteworthy, although I'm not sure why. It almost feels like a revelation. Here I am a widow, living alone, while COVID-19 is still holding us hostage, and I'm okay. I think about Danny; and I'm amused contemplating if he was alive and well during this time, I know exactly what he'd be doing. He would be fishing. There is no question about that. So either way, I'd be home alone.

April 24, 2020: The Day Before the 25th

Lori texted me earlier saying how it's "hard to believe tomorrow is nine months that Dan's been gone" and asked how I'm doing. She feels for me; that's comforting; that's friendship. I told her I thought about that last night, and I got a little weepy, but that still happens from time to time. Nine months. Feels more like nine weeks. Out of nowhere I think about the first time she met him and how she saw something in him that told her this could be the man for her friend. The memory of this brings an instant smile.

April 25, 2020

My friend, Maureen, and I went for a five-mile walk. We started these early morning walks last week and I'm so glad we did. I mentioned this significant date to her and asked if she felt the weight of Gary's passing with each month the first year since he passed, and she did. This helps me, in that if I feel it and she felt it, I'm sure many others have as well.

Once home, with coffee in hand, I let the tears come and then went to work in my garden. Later, Fran, Kalman, and I thought it would be fun to get subs from Dara's (their subs are the best), and we all enjoyed being together. It was a beautiful day, perfect for a "social distancing" picnic. Then later in the evening, we reconvened for toasting marshmallows and playing all kinds of trivia games. This made today so much easier to bear. At one point, Kalman and Jon told a Danny story that had me laughing. Something about squirrels, which I won't go into.

May 2, 2020: Love Is Lovely, Let It Grow

This morning I was up bright and early and went walking with Maureen. What a beautiful warm, sunny day. I looked forward to working in my garden. Once home from our walk, I had my coffee, enjoyed a nice long chat with Lori, and then headed out back. Everything is beginning to flower. It's absolutely lovely. The ground was nice and soft due to the rain we had the past couple of days, making it easy to weed. I like getting lost in my thoughts while gardening, whether it's planting, weeding, or deciding on what perennials I'm going to adorn my garden with this year and what annuals I'm going to put in my planters.

As I'm digging, I let myself go back to all the spring and summer Saturdays of years past. We would be in the sunroom having our coffee, and Danny would ask me what my plans were for the day. And then he would say, "I'm going fitchen." No, that's not a misspell; that's what he would say. So we would go on with our plans and resume later on for dinner, usually his homemade pizza and a movie. Oftentimes he would come home from fishing and find me in the yard; and he'd say, "Hey, baby cakes. Waz up?" That always made me laugh.

I would then ask him how he made out fishing; and he would either say "It sucked. I got nothing" or "Wait until you see the fish I caught for you." What's funny was he didn't eat freshwater fish, but he preferred freshwater fishing to saltwater fishing, except when he went out on the ocean on George's boat (our neighbor, George). He loved that, because he loved being out on a boat with good friends (he wasn't a fan of those party boats that hosted a big group of guys, most of whom he didn't know). I thought it was quite remarkable that he could cook something so yummy, that he himself wouldn't eat, as he only liked shellfish.

The other scenario would be when he planned to play golf with his good friend, Steve. If it was a golf day, his clubs would be all ready by the front door the night before. He was like a little boy when it came to meeting Steve to play golf. It was a combination of him loving the game and his friendship with Steve. He would even have me help pick out his golf outfit...of course.

The smell in the air reminds me of him and I'm mixed with feeling sad at what's no longer, but oddly enough feeling grateful that I have wonderful memories of this man who so often filled my heart with a million smiles.

It's almost eight o'clock PM, and I'm looking forward to being with my neighborhood family for another social distancing gathering around the firepit tonight. I can't wait until hugging is allowed again. Now there's a sentence I never thought I'd say.

May 6, 2020: Across the Great Divide

This morning while walking with Maureen, we got to talking about our husbands. Her husband, Gary, passed away eight and a half years ago, and I appreciate being able to bounce things off her. I was telling her about the morning I heard Danny call out to me and the disturbing effect it left. I mentioned to her how many people think that he was reaching out to me, and how I don't believe that, and she agreed with me. So many people think or feel that our loved ones watch over us, appear to us, or speak to us. But there is nothing to base this on, just feelings, which can be very deceiving. I'm a realist, so I base things on what I know according to what the Bible has to say about this. Then she said something very interesting. She feels "God doesn't allow that communication to continue after death so that we can move on." Makes sense to me.

What was also curious is she asked me if I dreamt about Danny; and I told her of my most recent very short, dream. I also mentioned that I had a dream about him months ago, but that was slightly disturbing, in that he didn't talk. We were sitting across a table from each other, and I told him I really missed him. And he just stared at me. She had a similar dream about Gary. She said they met at a crossroads; and neither of them said anything. They just stood and looked at each other. What is that, we wondered?

My pastor had this to say about those who think the dead are reaching out to us: "When a person passes, there's a gap between where they are and where we are here, and they can't bridge that gap." In addition he referenced Luke 16:1931, which makes all of this quite clear. He added, "The *Lord* forbids anybody to represent the dead." So you may want to rethink that visit to a fortune-teller.

Still curious I did a Google search; and I came upon a pastor who had this to say, "Mortals do not have the power of resurrection. Even people inspired by the devil cannot communicate with the dead." He went much deeper; but suffice it to say, it confirmed my initial feeling. That was not Danny. If you recall, I felt rattled and upset the entire day. I know he wouldn't have caused that.

May 10, 2020: Mother's Day

This morning I got up early, did some chores, ran an errand, and was back in time for the 10:30 AM livestream service from my church. Afterward, I drove to my mother-in-law's to bring her a gift. Sadly, because of the quarantine, we're not allowed in the building. It's a safety precaution to protect all the residents living in the Piscataway Senior Citizen Center.

Unfortunately, because it was so windy and chilly, we weren't even able to sit outside for even a few minutes. So we told each other we love each other. I handed off her gift to her as if we were in some quasi relay race, blew her a kiss, and left. Of course I began to cry. Irene is so strong, so vibrant, and so full of life, but she lost her son. And she can't even have her family come by for a proper visit, on Mother's Day.

I often forget that I'm a mom, well sort of. No, I never gave birth, but I don't believe that makes me any less a mom. Then I really started crying wondering if when Danny entered heaven how long before he was introduced to our child, the one I miscarried all those years ago. I envision his awe-struck face bursting with more love than either of us has ever been given the privilege to experience here on earth.

And then later today my sister, Marylou, sent me a text saying, "It occurred to me that one day you and I are going to meet the babies we miscarried. Isn't that amazing? For now, we will have to hope that Danny doesn't spoil them!" I laugh, just the thought of this makes me so happy.

Picture This

My husband had his wallet stolen three times and each time he got it back, which I find amazing. What really bothered him more than losing money, his credit cards, or his ATM card was he could not replace this picture of me, which for some reason was his favorite. I once asked him why, out of all the pictures of me, this one; and he said, "I just like it." Hmmm, go figure.

Every now and then, when I walk from room to room, I look about at those things that make up a room. Each piece of furniture, rugs, pictures, prints, art, sketches, and mirrors. All were just things before we made them a part of our home, all chosen for various reasons. Each piece conveyed our personalities individually and together. It was a collaboration and it was fun. I recently had two of the original blueprints of this house framed and determined that someday someone else will own this home and those two prints will be a gift to them.

Even when it came to buy this house. I figured out what we could afford, which was $160,000 not a penny more. We signed up with a couple of realtors (we were both in sales, so we were open to living in different counties in New Jersey). After looking at fifteen houses (yes, I kept track), we finally found the one. Well I found it with the help of a childhood friend who was a realtor. You see, when we started house hunting, if Danny didn't like what he saw on the outside, he would tell the realtor he wasn't going in. You can imagine how this thrilled them. He didn't like his time wasted, especially if it was baseball season, or basketball season, or football season (you could also throw in hockey and golf). He really liked sports. So he told me to check out potential homes first; and if it was worth him seeing it, then he would come back with me. So that's what I did.

When I saw this house, I knew it was the one. It's a lovely house, a center hall colonial built in 1938 with so much character and in excellent condition. It's on a very pretty and quiet street and had three bedrooms and a basement with a high ceiling (he was 6'2" so this was important). It had all that and then some. However, it was priced at $179,900, way over our budget. When he saw it, he liked it as much as I did. So he said let's offer $155,000. I questioned this low-ball offer, but I trusted both God and him, and we put in the offer. Guess what the owner countered with? Yup, $160,000, which was exactly what I had originally budgeted.

Many of the things we bought have a story, not a particularly fascinating story but a story, nonetheless. These are sweet memories and I enjoy getting lost in thought as I recall them.

May 21, 2020: The Worst "First"

This was the "first" I had been dreading. What I didn't expect was that on Tuesday of this week, May 19, I cried on and off all day long. I just could not get a grip. It started while I was working. It seemed the 21st kept coming up for meetings, whether moving meetings, changing meetings, and canceling meetings all related to May 21. Yesterday was better, but just a reminder that I still had to face today, what would have been our twenty-sixth anniversary.

The realization is that for the first time in twenty-six years, I will not be donning my wedding dress. I will not be anticipating seeing Danny's face at the sight of me in my gown and hearing his delightfully infectious laugh. This realization jerks at my heart in a way that causes me to barely be able breath.

It's over; and as I'm typing this, the tears are flowing. But I think to myself, "We had a good run with this anniversary celebration." The donning of the dress made our anniversary so special. No fancy dinner, bouquet of roses, or piece of jewelry could ever hold a candle to the glee that dress brought. You might say it was a magical dress!

So in anticipation of what I'd be facing today, Fran has rallied the girls (Estrella, Gabbie, and Ileana) for a girl's night. To start the day, I went to Fran's earlier this morning for coffee. And we broke all social distancing rules, because she knew a hug was needed, which it was, and it was so healing. Later we all took a leisurely walk, then pizza, wine, and friendship. The thought of being alone tonight was daunting, and Fran knew it. She said, "Being there for those you love is like breathing. You don't have to think about it."

I am most grateful for the humility I feel because of the blessings in my life and pray that God will always keep me humble.

June 14, 2020

After church service, I met up with my friend, Cindy. It's been months since we've been able to get together due to the quarantine; but now that the parks have reopened, we planned to meet up for a 4.5-mile walk. It was great catching up and we talked for hours afterward on her front porch. Of course we talked about Danny, and she opened up his obituary online (I was touched that she did that). And we were looking through all the pictures that my brother-in-law, Ron, uploaded. I was telling her funny stories that came to mind, which she enjoyed hearing about. She, like everyone else who knew him, loved him. He really was so easy to love.

When I got back home, I went out to water my garden. As I was watering, I thought about the pictures on the website. The weight of his absence hits me, leaving me feeling this void. It all went so fast. Just then something Billy Graham said comes to mind. When asked what surprised him the most about life, he didn't hesitate to say, "The brevity of life." Well there you have it. No matter if you're here for thirty, sixty, or ninety years, it goes by so fast. I told Danny I wouldn't be ready to say goodbye to him if it was twenty years from now. Although given the choice, I would have taken twenty more years with him in an instant.

Where's Mark Cuban?

Several years ago people started noticing that Danny "looked like" Mark Cuban, even his mom, who was the first person to bring this to our attention. When I was asked what I thought, I could see some resemblance, but Danny was much more handsome. Not because he was my husband, but because it was true (I think Mark might agree).

Well a few years ago, Danny happened to be home when he ran into our mailman. He had me laughing hysterically as he was telling me how our mailman was saying, "Dude, has anyone ever told you, you look just like Mark Cuban? You rock, dude!" To hear Danny tell the story and the look on his face as he was telling me was so comical. And in the years going forward, every time Danny saw him, he would say, "Dude, you rock!" It made us both laugh.

So about a week ago, I was hanging out with Jon and Fran in their backyard and Jon went out front for something. When he came back, he said he saw our mailman, who asked him, "Where's Mark Cuban been?" At first Jon didn't know who he was talking about then he realized and had to tell him Dan passed away. I'm so glad I didn't see the look on his face when Jon told him. I want to chuckle when I think about how fascinated this man was that my husband so resembled Mark Cuban. Had I seen his face when he found out Danny was no longer with us, I'm afraid that would overshadow this humorous story.

June 25, 2020: The Swift Passage of Time

Today marks eleven months. Why on every month anniversary do I feel this pit in my stomach and become weepy? The answer to that is twofold. On one hand it initiates reflection on what we were doing just one year ago today. I was with my man, still hoping for a miracle and so happy for every opportunity to curl up next to him and cuddle. I had no idea what I would be facing and most of the time I didn't think about it.

On the other hand, it's a reminder of just how quickly time passes by. It's mystifying, isn't it? What I mean by that, without sounding all 1960s "heavy," is we can all remember turning twenty-five, as someone would inevitably point out that we were now a quarter of a century years old and how fast life has gone by since then (I had to look up sayings from the 1960s because I knew there was a word used to describe a serious subject). It seems "heavy" was the word of the decade.

Simply stated and according to Psalm 144:4 regarding life, "They (referring to us) are like a breath; their days are like a fleeting shadow."

The Perfect Trifecta

I would like to tell you that at this point in time, just two and a half weeks away from the one-year anniversary of Danny's death, I am stronger, I cry less, and I laugh more. Then there are days like this past Sunday, July 5, I cried on and off all day. Why? Well I looked back at occurrences that took place that reminded me I no longer had my man here to help me deal with things. And I only had to look as far back as a week or so ago: the shower backed up last week and water came dripping down through the kitchen ceiling; my new office chair came with such awful assembly instructions it caused me to cry out to God asking why he had taken my Danny so young, because he would have had this chair put together in no time; or the spin bike I ordered, once I put that together, I wasn't able to move the pedals (thankfully Kalman to the rescue); and last, but certainly not least, here I am, working from home when a storm came sweeping through town. I went to the kitchen and looked out the window only to find my neighbor's tree came down in my yard, just missing my house by a hair, all twenty-five feet of it!

Then I consider how after each of these incidents God showed me I am not alone. I had received a call or a text from my sister, a friend, my cousin, some funny, some inviting me to dinner, and some just texting to say they're thinking about me. And I would be remiss if I failed to mention when putting together the chair that, when I got stuck and unable to figure out what went where, I would ask God to please help me and he did.

Sunday evening my brother-in-law, Jimmy, called, and we had a really nice chat. After we hung up, Jon texted me to tell me Fran's friend, Ceese, was visiting; and she had flowers for me and Fran, just because she saw them and thought of us. So I happily went across the street to meet her for the first time and we spent a lovely time in Jon and Fran's backyard chatting. The day ended perfectly.

Facing every day with Jesus is what helps me through. I recall one of our favorite songs, "Can't Live A Day" *by Avalon*. Danny turned me on to their CD years ago. We'd be driving, and we would crank this song up and sing at the top of our lungs. There are many songs that speak to my heart, but none like this one. It is beautiful. You really should have a listen and be sure to turn up the volume to get the full effect.

So even though Sunday was tough, at this point in time, I can honestly say I am stronger, I cry less, and I laugh more. I love to laugh. I cannot imagine my life without Jesus and laughter (and ravioli and key lime pie).

July 25, 2020: One Year Later

"You and Me"

With arms wrapped around me, you'd look at me and say,
"Honey, when I'm gone, are you gonna be okay?"
At the time I couldn't imagine just how my life would be,
facing everyday no longer you and me.
I told you not at first, that much I knew for sure,
and now it's one year later and I've managed to endure.

They say the first year is the hardest, as I'm faced with all the firsts;
and out of all of those special days, our anniversary was the worst.
As it was approaching, dreading how it'd be,
I faced the day head on, no longer you and me.

With all the firsts behind me, except for this one here,
I realize with the help of God I have nothing to fear.
But it isn't fear that grips me, now I clearly see.
It's navigating life, no longer you and me.

I've made a lot of progress, babe, I'm going to be fine,
and the memories you left me with I'll cherish for all time.
We had that something special, which I'll hold dear for eternity,
and I'll always be so grateful that there was a you and me.

Kathleen A. Nawojczyk (July 19, 2020)

Only six tissues were used in the writing of this poem. I consider this progress.

The First Sendoff: August 1, 2020

Today my neighborhood family and I set sail on George's boat to spread Danny's ashes out to the sea. We had planned on doing this on July 25, as this is the one-year anniversary of his death; but that day wasn't good for everyone, so we pushed it out a week.

It was an absolutely beautiful day and I was feeling so humbled that my friends wanted to do this with me, that's love.

Before I spread his ashes, I looked at my friends, my genuine, loving, and beautiful friends, and I felt compelled to share this with them. I told them that, at times, when Danny and I would be discussing money (always his least favorite subject), he would often say, "Kath, I have no desire to be the richest man in the cemetery." He could care less about being "rich." Needless to say, according to the world's standards, he was not a wealthy man. However, if you combine the love and admiration he had from all of his friends and family, he was a very rich man. There is no end to the love these friends continue to express. I also reminded them how much he loved them and how often he would tell others of the "great neighbors we have."

Spreading his ashes gave me a feeling of honor as I watched them flow amidst the ocean breeze, freeing them from the confinement of the spreading urn. I wore a long white sundress (one of Danny's favorites); and Fran said even that added to the beauty of the occasion, as it too flowed through the breeze.

The moment the last of his ashes were gone, a fish appeared on the radar screen. Was it a sign? Some would say yes, I don't think so. But it was a sweet moment that brought smiles all around. The sunset was breathtaking as well. It was a lovely day and I am feeling uplifted.

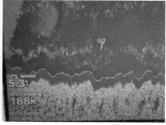

Continuing Education

Recently I attended a one-day retreat with the ladies from my Bible study. The topic was from a book written by Laura Story, entitled *When God Doesn't Fix It: Lessons You Never Wanted to Learn, Truths You Can't Live Without*. It really doesn't hit much closer to home for me than that. I gained much from this study.

This was another stepping stone in the healing process for me. I've been with many of these ladies for years; I count it a privilege to be among them. There was so much packed into this day, and I especially benefited from the breakout discussions. Listening to the testimonies and challenges some faced or are facing is one thing. However, it is their unshakeable faith that carries them, and I am in awe. While I will not elaborate specifically on any one of their situations (what is discussed in Bible study is confidential), suffice it to say, I felt a sense of honor that they bravely shared so deeply, trusting so easily. I shared as well, wanting them to know that during the grieving process God is healing my heart more and more each day. I feel a sense of responsibility to be encouraging, as others have been encouraging to me.

At one point we had a scavenger hunt and that was a fun, much-needed break that brought a lot of laughter. It became very competitive which caused me and my teammate, Debbie, to be very creative. We actually tied for first place against the very competitive Team Monica. Monica is a pastor's wife and fierce contender, which is not surprising, as all of the pastor's wives I know are strong, independent women, who I admire greatly.

All in all, a great day. I welcome these opportunities for growth. I never know what they will bring to my life, but I know it will be positive and inspiring.

How You Choose

We will all go through trials, that's just a given. We will all experience the intense pain of grief in our lives and most often not just once. It's how you choose to handle it, or more accurately it's how you accept it or not. If your nature is that of why me or poor me, the difficulty you will face in dealing with your loss will be paralyzing, and it will impede your healing. I believe dealing with great lose is the harshest reality we will ever have to face. But we all get to choose how we will deal with losing the loves in our lives.

To put this into perspective, ask yourself if, when your time on earth is through, do you want your loved ones be anchored to their heartache? To go through the rest of their lives in a constant state of sadness and/or misery because you are no longer here? Unless you're a narcissist or just really mean, I think the answer would be of course not. This causes me to wonder if narcissists know they're narcissists. I digress, it happens in the thought process.

Tomorrow Is Promised to No One

This past weekend was the nineteenth anniversary of 9/11. Every year I try to watch as much as possible of the reading of the names of those who perished. I feel they deserve to be remembered. It never gets easier to watch though, especially when I hear them read the name of a woman and her unborn child. That still brings stinging tears.

As I ponder these lives and the catastrophe that was 9/11 and I look back on all that has happened in the years following, including this year with the coronavirus, I began to contemplate just how much of life doesn't make sense. But is it meant to make sense? Where is it written that life is supposed to make sense? Some things in life need to make sense, such as math and science (my two worst subjects), but life itself, I dare say, more often than not, just doesn't make sense.

Perhaps God gave us this proverb for that very reason. *Proverbs 3:5–6* says, "Trust in the *Lord* with all your heart and lean not on your own understanding; in all your ways acknowledge him, and he will make your paths straight."

This is a helpful reminder, as many things in life confound me; but having God to lean on, well life really doesn't get more sound than that.

You're Not A Burden Either

Whenever the opportunity presents itself, I remind people who are facing challenges/trials to bring it immediately to God and leave it with him. What you are going through has not come as a surprise to him; and he understands more than anyone, your anxiety, your pain, and your hurts, to name a few. They will often tell me that they don't feel it's important enough to bring to God, as they feel he has much bigger issues to deal with: unrest in the Middle East, terrorism, earthquakes, and so on. Well, that's why he's God and we're not. I then tell them I pray for a good parking spot at the supermarket or mall on a nasty day and he always comes through. So if he provides me with a good parking space, you can trust he will carry you through anything you are facing, but you must place complete trust in him.

Is it always easy, no. It took me years to get into the practice of going to God before my mom, sisters, or friends. Sometimes I still bypass God and call one of my sisters or friends. And just to confuse you a bit, there are times I feel God places someone on my heart to reach out to (depending on the circumstance), and I'm comforted by them. But once you get yourself in the habit, just like anything else, it becomes second nature. You'll know if he's guiding you to reach out to a trusted family member or friend or if he wants you to wait on and rest in him.

Just as my husband was never a burden to me, we are not burdens to our loving God. He loves us with more love than all of our loved ones combined, and he wants us to "Cast all your anxiety on him because he cares for you" (*1 Peter 5:7*).

The Gift of Hope

Over the past few weeks, I have heard the word *hope* mentioned almost daily. It became difficult to ignore and so I felt nudged by God to speak on this.

What came to mind is that it was hope that motivated Danny to continue with yet another chemo treatment, even after receiving a terminal diagnosis. I too had hope; and that hope gave us a several months of delightfully memorable times with family and friends, special moments, and a lot of much-needed laughter.

Most of us have heard the expression "hope springs eternal" and many of us have seen the movie *Hope Floats*. There are several phrases that refer to hope; one I often use is "where there's life, there's hope." The Bible is filled with verses about hope. Many people have been given the name *Hope*. There is even a piece of furniture called a hope chest. We can remember as far back as when we were little kids trying to convince someone of something by saying, "Cross my heart and hope to die." In kids' world, it doesn't get much more serious than that.

Danny's favorite Bible verse was *Jeremiah 29:11*: "'For I know the plans I have for you,' declares the Lord, 'plans to prosper you and not to harm you, plans to give you hope and a future.'"

There is never a reason to abandon hope. Even if things don't turn out the way you had, dare I say, hoped. Think about what that hope did for you and those around you. Hope is a gift, one to be cherished and one to be shared. Hope is not wishful thinking (wishes are for birthday candles). I found this online:

> Hope discovers what can be done instead of grumbling about what cannot be done. Hope draws its power from a deep trust in God and the basic goodness of mankind. Hope regards problems, small or large, as opportunities. Hope cherishes no illusions, nor does it yield to cynicism. (getouttheboxinspiration.wordpress.com/March 16, 2011)

I think even pessimists must have some fragment of hope, no matter how bleak their outlook is on just about everything...at least I hope so.

No Way to Know

As I lay in bed one night, out of nowhere, I thought about when Danny proposed, which prompted me to get up and slip on my engagement ring. I stopped wearing it just a few months after the one-year anniversary of his death. I just stared at it remembering how wonderful it felt, how that precious ring told the world that Daniel Richard Nawojczyk loved me so much that he wanted to spend the rest of his life with me. How could I have known that the rest of his life wouldn't be the rest of my life. How could I have known we would only celebrate twenty-five wedding anniversaries. I could go on and on, but I'll spare you all the only twenty-fives we celebrated.

The reality is I couldn't have known nor should I have known. These things are not meant to be known. We're meant to live life day by day not for all the tomorrows. If we did, well, that's not living, that's just existing, and there's far too much living to do.

Full disclosure, I'm still wearing my wedding band…baby steps.

Sharing the Honor

A couple of weeks back, I visited with my mother-in-law. We had such a nice time together; she is truly an amazing woman. At 93 years old, she continues to embrace life and all it has to offer her. After we had lunch and before we were to meet with her two best girlfriends for a walk in the fresh air, I asked her if she would like to spread the rest of Danny's ashes when we get together in a couple of weeks. The look on her face lifted my heart. She asked me if I was sure, which I was, and she said she would be honored. I knew she would be; and as his mom, I felt it was the right thing to do. I explained to her that when I was spreading his ashes, I also felt it an honor. The gratitude on her face told me I had given her a gift. It was a pretty special moment.

The Final Sendoff

It's Halloween, and today is the day we chose to spread the rest of Danny's ashes. Our family gathering consisted of my mother-in-law, Irene; Danny's siblings: Ronnie and his wife, Monica; Danny's younger brother, Jimmy, and his wife, Susan, and their son, Gregory; Carolyn and her daughters, Candace and Casey, and Casey's husband, Dan; and myself. His sister, Diana, and her husband, Aaron, live in Missouri, so unfortunately they and their children were understandably unable to be with us.

The weather had been horrendous the past two days, as it was cold and rainy. Today the weather report predicted the temperature would be forty-eight degrees and sunny with ten-to-twenty-mile-an-hour winds. This causes the picture in my head of his ashes floating gently above the ocean waves to change dramatically.

I was feeling emotional on the drive down to meet everyone. I kept envisioning Irene spreading her son's ashes and my heart was feeling heavy at the thought. Once there, I looked around at everyone and knew, once again, we were all in this together. No matter all the times each of us individually have grieved, today we would bid him a final farewell together.

The meeting place was set at the beach end of Dover Avenue in Lavallette, which was right at the border where Ortley Beach begins. According to Ronnie, they spent many happy times there, and that makes me smile. What also brought a smile was seeing that a few of us were wearing clothes that were once Danny's, which I felt was a thoughtful homage to this much-loved man.

The weather turned out to be absolutely beautiful, which was pretty amazing. The sun was shining down all around us, and it felt more like sixty-five degrees; and if there were ten-to-twenty-mile-an-hour winds, they seemed to have bypassed us.

When it came time for Irene to spread his ashes, I realized there was far too much for her to spread by herself, not to mention the weight of the spreading urn, so we thought it would be best if whoever wanted to take part in this could. Watching everyone take turns was so moving. When it was my turn, I was overcome with emotion and once again I let the tears flow. Last, but certainly not least, Ronnie gave the ultimate tribute by bringing the last of Danny's ashes directly into the ocean. He had conveniently worn his bathing suit under his clothes and proceeded to walk then run unwaveringly into the oncoming waves...the perfect way to end the spreading of our Danny's ashes.

It brought to mind the many years we'd all get together the day after Christmas and did what became known as *The Nawojczyk Plunge*. Ron and Monica would come up from North Carolina for Christmas; and they would rent a house on the beach in Long Beach Island (aka LBI), the week between Christmas and just before New Year's Eve. The rules were simple. You had to wear a bathing suit, no wet suits allowed, and you had to go all the way under. I think it was the first year we did it when Danny wore his sandals which were more like open sneakers; and the suction made it difficult for him to pick his feet up, so he was having a heck of a time trying to get out of the ocean. I was laughing so hard watching him and just shaking my head, thinking, only Danny. These are the memories that will keep me laughing; these are the memories I delight in.

Afterward, we all got in our cars and reconvened at the Lavallette Gazebo just a short distance from where we were, but on the bay side. While enjoying lunch, we told Danny stories and just chatted about whatever came up. The laughter all around was music to my ears. The sun continued to shine down on us, and we could not have been more grateful for the beautiful day. At one point I asked Irene how she felt. Understandably she was filled with emotion but said, "I can't believe how much ashes there were. I think he must have gained weight!" I love this woman.

This man's life touched so many lives in ways that made all of us better for having known him. He brought laughter to the hearts of many... this one life. I keep pondering that thought. If it wasn't for the life of Daniel Richard Nawojczyk, how very different all of our lives would be.

I'm grateful that his Mom's generation, generally speaking, chose life.

You and Me

This photo was taken on September 15, 2001, just four days after 9/11. We were going to his class reunion.

No, the positioning of me under the shrimp sign was not strategically done on purpose!

At the US Open. My champion!

Honeymoon in Jamaica (1994)

Jamaica (January 2019)

Irene's ninetieth birthday bash. A wonderful time was had by all!

One of the things I loved about him was how much he loved his family. I believe that says a lot about a man.

Two days after his mom's ninetieth birthday, September of 2017, he was diagnosed with cancer. One day he's serving wine to his mom's friends in celebration of her milestone birthday, and two days later a visit to his doctor changed the course of our lives.

At our wedding   At Ron and Monica's
                        wedding

Worth Fighting For

As I look back on our marriage, I am thankful that we fought together, with God, through every challenge, never giving up on each other because we were worth fighting for. Had I left him because of his drug addiction, what would have happened to him? What would have happened to me for that matter? We had survived that awful time and came through it stronger. We survived a miscarriage, my only pregnancy, but we held each other up. And again, we came through it. We loved, we laughed, and just to keep things interesting we even fought. We had that something special, that bond that could not be broken. That bond I dreamed of having so long ago.

This is what I wrote in my last anniversary card to him:

> Twenty-five years ago, we vowed, before God, family, and friends, to have and to hold, from this day forward, for better, for worse, for richer, for poorer, in sickness, and in health…and we kept those promises. What I never expected was that I would love you more deeply than I ever thought possible. I believe that's because we made each other better in so many ways. And, when met with life's challenges (and we've had our share), we rose up together and fought for us, because we knew we were worth fighting for. Twenty-five years later, I love you truly, madly, deeply.

I'll never forget what a priest said at the wedding of a friend, well over thirty-five years ago. He said, "May you love each other the least amount today." I was young, and initially I didn't quite grasp it. But as I matured, and with each wedding I attended, I always recalled his words. Then it happened to us. We loved each other the least amount on May 21, 1994.

Ours will go down in history as one of the greatest love stories of all time. Why, you ask? Because it's ours. After all, this is how everyone should feel about their love.

An Unanswerable Question

I've been asked if I would consider dating, down the road. The idea doesn't appeal to me, not yet anyway. That said, rarely do lines from a movie stay with me. Not unless they're curiously profound. But one night while watching a Hallmark movie, this line struck me, so I wrote it down. One of the main characters had this to say about a broken heart: "I like to think that a broken heart can be healed and that a healed heart can love deeper and more fully than ever before."

I would like to think that too. The cover of my journal resonates.

About the Author

Kathleen A. Nawojczyk grew up Kathleen Prillo in Elizabeth, New Jersey. She is the third of four children born to Anthony and Josephine Prillo. After graduating from Mother Seton Regional High School in Clark, New Jersey, she started working for a major pharmaceutical company. However, after ten years she was given an opportunity to go into sales. Selling window treatments on the wholesale side felt right to her, as she is very much a people  person. It was during this time she was setup on a blind date with Dan Nawojczyk; they hit it off, fell in love, and were married two years later.

After fourteen years of working in sales, the driving was beginning to take its toll. She was given an opportunity to return to the same pharmaceutical company she had left years earlier. She continues to work there to this day as an Executive Assistant. She has also acquired her Mad Dogg Spin Instructor Certification as well as ACE Strength and Conditioning Certification and now teaches spin and weight classes.

She has always enjoyed writing short stories and poems for her own pleasure.

CPSIA information can be obtained
at www.ICGtesting.com
Printed in the USA
BVHW021039140621
609525BV00011B/340/J